CRITICISM AND PERSONAL TASTE

Criticism and
Personal Taste

BY

R. PEACOCK

CLARENDON PRESS · OXFORD

1972

Oxford University Press, Ely House, London W.1

GLASGOW NEW YORK TORONTO MELBOURNE WELLINGTON
CAPE TOWN IBADAN NAIROBI DAR ES SALAAM LUSAKA ADDIS ABABA
DELHI BOMBAY CALCUTTA MADRAS KARACHI LAHORE DACCA
KUALA LUMPUR SINGAPORE HONG KONG TOKYO

PN
81
P4

61600

PRINTED IN GREAT BRITAIN BY
HAZELL WATSON AND VINEY LTD
AYLESBURY, BUCKS

PREFACE

THE two parts of this book are complementary to each other, without being in logical sequence. The first part avoids the notion of a single thing called criticism and attempts instead to distinguish a group of critical thinking processes and the influence that the real conditions of individual taste have on them. The manner in which varied reactions and taste play havoc with reason and aesthetic standards is a permanent problem. I have attempted a fresh approach by emphasizing, against the strong tendency to isolate for argument an intensive poetic or literary-aesthetic ideal, the great variety of literary works, and by replacing what one might call aesthetic monism with the notion that poems and literary works may have a number of different functions for the individual reader. The second part of the book is based on a distinction between the range of 'values', almost infinite in number, which may be present in literature and are the object of very intricate assessment, and a relatively restricted number of primary criteria of judgement, which may be looked on as essential for all works.

The study is addressed to anyone who is deeply exercised by the problem of taste, by the insistent reality of individual liking and disliking, and the claim for freedom of choice that makes itself felt in the aesthetic as in other spheres. There are remarkably few books that deal with basic problems of judgement. It may be that scholars consider the primary aspects of judgement too simple to be worth putting down; or it may be they share a general scepticism about criteria, and follow the habit that favours doing some practical criticism and letting principles look after themselves. In the United States the so-called New Criticism has certainly produced new critical theories and terms of great vitality and force, but so numerous, and often of such individual character, that they reward the specialist in poetics or literary aesthetics more than the inquirer after first principles of judgement. I hope this book will be of interest as a commentary on a number of provocative problems arising both from basic difficulties of judgement and from the more difficult questions of taste.

CONTENTS

PART I

1

THE PROBLEM OF TASTE

The theme of this study is individual taste and its relation to criticism. They are too deeply involved with each other for comfort. Criticism is, for the experienced reader, founded in taste, whilst taste is normally developed with the help of criticism. In exploring this reciprocal relationship I wish to carry the argument a stage beyond the most customary treatments that centre on the nature and function of criticism alone. These often have the effect, whether intended or not, of putting criticism into the up-stage position, and pushing literature and taste down-stage. Of course criticism is always presented, by ideal intention, as in the service of literature; it should help readers to discrimination and understanding. But as professional critics and teachers we are often in danger of shifting the focus of values heedlessly from the literary source to the critical act; saying, in effect, that the values of literature emerge as and when approved and elucidated by ourselves. Yet professional critics and scholars, if they step for a moment outside their absorption, must face the fact that whilst they speak to thousands, literature itself in effect speaks to hundreds of thousands and performs a function that is independent of a rigorous professional criticism. I shall base my argument on this liberty of literature to *function* for very large numbers of individuals, and furthermore in different ways for different individuals.

Before broaching the problem of taste directly, some brief provisional comments on criticism might help to clear the ground. The word in English does variant and ubiquitous service; we use it and make it mean different things according to the context or the moment. It can mean appreciation, but it can also mean denigration; it can mean a philosophical, or an aesthetic, assessment; it can include historical problems, but need not. It includes both the simpler notion of a judgement and also the very complex procedures of detailed evaluation. Judgement, criticism, and evaluation are overlapping terms, but far from being identical.

A particular note was introduced in the last generation by Richards's term 'practical criticism', and the idea of something practical, as against abstract thought, is always attractive in this country. Practical criticism caught on and has been exercised with a view to detailed analysis of works, elaborated into reasoned statements about success and failure (of whole or part), but also into full interpretation of historical classics. Here empirical methods are the norm, as case-law is in the legal field. This extends to ideas about criticism itself. The abstractions of theory are often intensely disliked; the majority tend to the view that you can't say what criticism is, you just take it as it comes.

Since none of the main terms are really defined, it would be futile to attempt to get logical tidiness into their use. Simple primary judgements, such as that a new poem obviously has some good points, soon merge into criticism of a more detailed kind; and the former, though apparently immediate, are really based on very rapid apprehensions by a skilled practitioner; they are not a different kind of mental process, but essentially similar to the slower processes of assessment. Evaluation is a sophisticated variant of both judgement and criticism; its virtue lies in eliminating the ambiguity of the traditional words, which serve both positives and negatives. Evaluation, considered as skilled assessment, implies something worth the exercise.

Nevertheless, certain things are without doubt obscured by the term 'criticism' being also used to cover the vast amount of academic work connected with study of literature, work which includes numerous historical problems and which deals not with new or dubious works but with accepted classics. I think we should distinguish radically between the primary act of judgement—has this work some literary quality and why?—and the complexities of sophisticated critical argument about established works, works that have been, as far as we are concerned, already judged and given a place amongst what are called the classics. Such argument hammers out detailed discrimination, taking all the factors, including history, into account. The field of discussion, covering a large number of value-problems and affiliations of literature, is almost unlimited, human variation being what it is. But all this intricacy of critical scholarship does not remove the prior act of deciding whether a work is within the pale of aesthetic value or not. From this exercise we should also distinguish the teaching of appreciation of literary classics, in which prior judgements are accepted; this processs is really an explanation, rather than a making, of critical judgements.

In a world in which 'criticism' has become so much a baggy, portmanteau word it is helpful to divide the mass of literature provisionally into the newer, the contemporary, the emergent, and the past, established classics. Judgement, in the sense of a verdict on quality, is at least more obviously relevant to the newer works, though not exclusively, whilst interpretative-evaluative criticism is directed more frequently to classics. Negative judgements on the latter are precarious; there is something slightly foolish about trying to kill horses that have been alive for ages. You can't displace literature that has once made its mark; you can only assert your personal dislike or puzzlement, or suggest why you think its meaning has faded. But new works are different. Whenever we read one we come face to face with primary judgement-making. Is it worth taking seriously? Is it good? Or, on a second look: were my first reactions justified? It is in connection with this problem that primary criteria are relevant and legitimate.

This distinction made, we can deal more practically with the problem of criteria, admittedly a teasing one. It is common nowadays, in view of the enormous variety of literary forms, even within the broad kinds of lyric, drama, and fiction, to say that all prescriptive judging belongs to a past age, that each new work embodies more likely than not the principle by which it should be judged, and that, in short, no conditions, let alone rules, can be laid down with any hope that they would be valid. Or it is said, alternatively, that the few positive criteria that could safely be put forward are so elementary and broad as to be wholly uninteresting. Whilst agreeing that to have a little pack of criteria ready to hand and to apply them regularly with each act of judgement would be monotonous and even inane, we cannot deny, if we are honest, that criteria are in our mind somewhere, as we assess; they are established influences, presences, forces; we do rely on them, without necessarily invoking them by name. Critics who are impatient of them have perhaps forgotten that at some stage they learned, or were taught, to observe certain features that appear regularly in good works (e.g. appropriate images, good composition, unity of effect, etc.). What they do in practice, to judge whether a work new to them has the right look, is to use the negatives: it is badly composed, there is no unified relation between plot and idea, the rhymes are bad, the metaphors are mixed, the style is bare and lacklustre, and so on. If these expressions convey what is wrong, the implication is that their positive opposites (good composition, unity, vivid style, etc.) represent the qualities missing. Listed, they would constitute in effect a code of rules. Thus criteria are undoubtedly implied, and essentially, though obliquely, brought into play. I myself think that it is worth while putting forward in positive, direct form a few basic criteria. Hence I have discussed in Part II of this book what may be held to be some of the salient factors in judgement at the present time.

In a general way I believe that by the use of such criteria, and with the backing of sufficient experience of reading, it is possible to establish fairly safe preliminary judgements about the claims of works, especially new works, to the possession of some literary quality; and by this I mean judgements that will command wide agreement, even though one has to admit that specious works often slip by and have a temporary success. The crucial stage of disagreement, of sharply differing reactions and assessments amongst experienced critics, begins, I think, with the detailed analysis which entails the evaluation of *all* the elements involved. For it is then that many more factors, including beliefs, philosophical views, and stylistic preferences, come into full play.

At this stage, too, arises the problem of personal taste, which is the main theme of the following pages.

The argument must start from the real fact of a personal taste. I mean by this not simply 'my taste', a taste that anyone, educated or ill-educated, can have, but the fact of personal taste within the area of an accepted good art. In literature, I mean the fact that one person prefers Henry James, and another Dickens or D. H. Lawrence; that one person likes Keats and Tennyson more than Wordsworth or Browning. So that really the problem I want to investigate here concerns not the question: what is a good piece of literature?—but, given a good piece of literature, why does one person like it, and another not? And why are so-called universal judgements not really so, and yet valid?

The problem of taste is rarely stated in a direct way; it is circumvented. Criticism has always been represented as the business of judging a work to be good, bad, or indifferent; and it was assumed that different judgements meant one of two things: either that one of the judgements was deficient and one of the parties wrong; or that there exists an area of reactions which are capricious and beyond rational explanation. It is true that people often say you can know what is good without liking it. We recall how Brunetière said to an impressionistic critic: You always praise what you like, I never do. This is the declaration of the serious critic endeavouring to eliminate personal idiosyncrasies from his judgement of a work of literature, and reproaching another critic for simply indulging his taste. Many people hold the view, implied by Brunetière's comment, that these two positions are irreconcilable; either your judgement is impersonal and pure, or it is biased and impure. But the problem of likes, taste, and judgement is not so easily shelved. I think a doubt can be raised about this way of 'knowing what is good'. The lack of spontaneous response, of surging aesthetic pleasure, is surely a barrier of a kind; it prevents really full knowledge; and without full knowledge can one really be said to know well enough to say a work is good?

Against this I want to put forward the view that these two positions are not in fact so rigidly opposed as they have mostly appeared to be. It is a simple fact that we have favourite poets and writers, those we like more, without necessarily disliking all others. It seems to me that there must be a better reason for this than simply the idea of capricious or unaccountable personal tastes. This is a matter where I find it useful, as often in aesthetic matters, to bear in mind the attitudes of writers themselves. Whilst The Critic, putting on his mask of public, impersonal adjudicator, looks at all literature for poetic enjoyment, for 'the art', the poet instinctively disregards a vast amount. All artists have most decided preferences; I think it could be said that artists as a class have many more blind spots than ordinary people who are the recipients and not the creators of art. But

who would say that artists do not have good taste, good judgement? The question sounds absurd. It will be part of my argument that there are not two classes of people interested in
literature, on the one hand the creators, with strong and wilful
tastes, and on the other hand the recipients, who are expected to
show universal appreciation; but that there are for everyone
varying degrees of recipiency, varying reactions, varying
defections, of taste, all of which are equally justified. It is
possible for some people to have a very catholic taste, but for
others to have very pronounced tastes; to maintain such pronounced tastes is fully justified and in no way a disability. Good
taste does not depend on catholic taste. I would say that people
with pronounced tastes might well be much nearer in their
sensibility to creative artists themselves, and that their disposition to pronounced tastes may well be connected with strong
features of personality, intellectual or otherwise.

This is not the traditional way of thinking. A good example
of tradition would be Hume.[1] The essay 'Of the Standard of
Taste' uses the eighteenth-century concept of taste in the sense
of 'good taste', the 'principles' of which he takes almost as a
matter of course to be 'universal'. They are to be observed
particularly in 'those works that have survived all the caprices of
mode and fashion, all the mistakes of ignorance and envy', and
in the 'durable admiration' accorded to them. Philosophers
yield to each other successively, but with poets it is different;
they maintain their empire and prove that there is a standard of
taste, which simply imposes itself. The process depends on men
of sense refining their observation by 'practice', constantly
comparing works, and removing all 'prejudice' from their minds;
in this way the best inevitably comes floating to the top and is
seen in its superlative quality. Variable judgements issue therefore mainly from faults in those who judge; the equipment of the
critics is defective. 'The general principles of taste are uniform in
human nature: where men vary in their judgements, some
defect or perversion in the faculties may commonly be re-
marked.'

[1] Hume's attempt to acknowledge the natural origins of difference of taste and
yet to justify a rational 'standard of taste' has been recently discussed by H.
Osborne, 'Hume's Standard and the Diversity of Taste', *British Journal of Aesthetics*,
7, No. i (1967), pp. 50–6, and P. Kivy, 'Hume's Standard of Taste: Breaking
the Circle', ibid., pp. 57–66.

But Hume makes a notable concession which is important for my later argument. He allows two sources, based in nature, of variation of taste, the one being the humours of particular men, the other, the particular manners of an age or country. Such diversity is 'blameless', so that here reason must allow that 'a certain degree of diversity in judgement is unavoidable, and we seek in vain for a standard, by which we can reconcile the contrary sentiments'. Thus young men may like the love poetry of Ovid, whilst the elderly prefer the philosophical Tacitus; or, according to our temper, we have a special sympathy with the writer who resembles us. Equally, the different kinds, tragedy, comedy, satire, have their partisans. Nevertheless, Hume is careful to contain such diversity; a preference on such grounds may not be allowed to involve condemnation of the other party; it is tolerated, allowed to exist, but not to be aggressive. Hume sticks to his main principle: 'It is plainly an error in a critic, to confine his approbation to one species or style of writing, and condemn all the rest.' Hume will not go against reason, but we feel that, although he makes his concessions, he does so in a spirit of resignation, and would really prefer not to have to do so.

The position today is very indeterminate, with almost a conspiracy to leave the problem of objective values or criteria severely alone, and in fact to behave as though one could have one's cake and eat it. The predominant practical attitude is permissive, if one may borrow the ethical analogy from other spheres of present-day life. People are generously allowed their 'opinion', and above all their 'right' to have personal opinions. And one reserves the right to have one's own principles, without foisting them on to others, and also often without being in any hurry to define or declare them. In consequence the ghost of Hume is still about, though the emphases have perhaps changed places. He believed firmly in good taste, and allowed room for individualist aberrations that in time became in fact the basis of new notions;[1] today we believe firmly in individual variety, but leave room in the back of our thoughts for a standard that would be necessary to prevent a pure chaos of voices, the ultimate separation of each from all. We cannot use 'good taste' today with the certainty and absoluteness of Hume; we restrict it to the role of a minor compliment ('he has good taste'). But

[1] Cf. T. Brunius, *David Hume on Criticism* (Uppsala, 1952).

although we can see that Hume's concessions were anticipations of trends later to become marked, his main view of a literature characterized by 'universal' values is still vaguely in the picture, accepted, if not explicitly and literally, then implicitly, as a felt bulwark against total individual diversity. Relativism has not been eagerly accepted, at least not as an argued position, except by a few; and those few, like Mr. Heyl, have to be in-fighters for their case.[1] I do not mean that everyone is expected to be able to read everything with equal assent, which is absurd. The implication in the air is different; it is that if one *could* read everything, one *should*, ideally, be able to arrive at a positive judgement of everything that anyone else had ever put into the canon, *unless there is a fault in oneself*. The implication is that only time stands in one's way to universal acceptance of good works.

These uncertainties pervade the arguments, for instance, of Mr. Righter in his *Logic and Criticism*,[2] which deserves acknowledgement as a serious attempt to come to terms with the present situation. It is difficult not to agree with Mr. Righter on many points, especially on the difficulty, even undesirability, of devising too precise critical concepts. But one cannot help but feel that it is insufficient just to describe, however accurately, the 'actual' character of critical activity; to me, after reading him, this looks like a great sea of waves ever in motion, amidst which you cannot know your bearings with certainty, and where you will certainly feel wet, yet you can with luck just keep your head above water, and see other heads at the same business. Mere acceptance of this situation leaves one with an empty feeling. We require more; we need a positive justification of it. We need an appreciation of the factors involved of a kind that suggests more sense in the whole thing. It must also be admitted that a more discriminating analysis of the various origins of differing opinion is called for. Mr. Righter, it seems to me, has the attitude, without specifically declaring it, that though personal variations in judgement are a matter of course they are extraneous to the value question. Like Hume, he sees them as natural but essentially as an unavoidable falling-short, as deficiencies of the individual in face of literary values that are

[1] Bernard C. Heyl, *New Bearings in Aesthetics and Art Criticism* (New Haven, Conn., 1943).
[2] William Righter, *Logic and Criticism* (London, 1963).

trans-individual. But in that case who decides the values? Some individual must make the start.

On this point too much influence has perhaps been allowed to the notion of the 'ideal' reader; one is supposed to have to posit something of the sort in order to be able to put forward any criticism of a piece of literature. It is of course part of the vexing problem of differing interpretations or 'readings', as well as of differing judgements. But the situation is similar to any in which the mind is concerned. The basic position is surely that any one human being is always a mixture of class properties and individual variations; whenever he thinks, or is a prey to passions, or takes decisions, what he thinks and feels and does is partly similar to what any other member of the human race, or of a clan, would think, feel, and do, and partly different by virtue of his individuality. In these arguments about readings and judgements and interpretations a theoretical strain is too often put upon this simple, natural situation. People begin to think that one must either be absolutely representative of a class or absolutely individual, or that there are principles of mind, and poetics, that are transcendent; they are not part of the creation of literary people, but have to be aspired to, and 'reached', by them. But it follows from the natural situation of variety that there will always be a measure of agreement, which is interesting, and a measure of variation, which is also interesting. It seems to me that here the biological principle is as good as any other: everything that is truly alive is a variant of the genus to which it belongs; this applies to the mental faculties as well and is one reason why we place so much stress in education on making people think for themselves. But variation carried to excess negates its own condition; it ceases to be variation and becomes something else, whereupon an entirely new situation is created. This may or may not develop further, but it is subject to a new set of conditions, the first being no longer relevant.

The view I wish to put forward is that individual variation in taste, which is a kind of selection and involves a variation of judgement, is not a failure to reach some grace of absolute literary insight, but is dynamic in essence and has positive character. The case is similar to that of religions, to take another example of a phenomenon with complex interactions of intellectual and emotional factors. Are there not some that are germane to our nature? And some that are alien, and perhaps even harmful? We do not expect a man to be a Mohammedan and a Christian at one and the same time. No doubt if he is one or the other he will have a primary understanding of religious feeling as a matter of religious need; but he will be either a Christian or a Mohammedan, and whichever he is will be a matter of much deeper insight to him than the other.

A starting point for argument may be found in reasons George Santayana gives against the doctrine that beauty in art should in principle claim absolute universal appreciation. He observes that such agreement on aesthetic matters as exists is based on similarity of origin, nature, and circumstance, which tends to bring about identity in all judgements and feelings. It is unmeaningful to say that what is beautiful to one man *ought* to be beautiful to another. If they react similarly by associations and disposition the same thing *will* be beautiful. If not, one will see unity and beauty, another a shapeless mass and ugliness; and you cannot say that what the latter *cannot* see 'ought' to be beautiful to him. What we mean by 'he ought to see this or that beauty' is that he would see it if his disposition and training were what our ideal demands for him. For instance, we take pleasure in having our own judgements supported by others; our own doubts are dissipated if our opinions are accepted universally. If we were secure we should accept freely the natural differences of feeling in others. But we are not, and so our ideal of other men tends to include the agreement of their judgements with our own. Hence we are unreasonable enough to require that all races should admire the same style of architecture and all ages the same poets.

This is untenable, says Santayana. 'Nothing has less to do with the real merit of a work of imagination than the capacity of all men to appreciate it; the true test is the degree and kind of satisfaction it can give to him who appreciates it most.' A symphony loses nothing because nine-tenths of mankind are deaf to it. Moreover, 'incapacity to appreciate certain types of beauty may be the condition *sine qua non* for the appreciation of another kind; the greatest capacity both for enjoyment and creation is highly specialized and exclusive, and hence the greatest ages of art have often been strangely intolerant'. Confidence in one's own intuition, proud assent of one's own taste, is the greatest evidence of aesthetic sincerity. 'If we (on the other hand) were less learned and less just, we might be more efficient. If our appreciation were less general, it might be more real, and if we trained our imagination into exclusiveness, it might attain to character.'

If we accept this powerful argument, if in principle we acknowledge a special kind of validity for personal taste, we may seem to have slipped back to the beginning of the problem and be begging the whole question, since seeking norms for criticism arises from the desire to escape from the anarchy of personal tastes. This is not, however, Santayana's position, because he implies all along group agreement at least, something lying, in fact, between the absolute universal and the absolutely singular.

This is a reasonable and acceptable view because, in the short or the long run, there must be some consensus of opinion about literary works, if these are in any sense to be public affairs. They are mostly written by men for men; they rest to some extent at least on common norms of linguistic meaning and reaction (even if they take time to penetrate); and are therefore social, in the broad sense. In this sphere, doubtless, almost nothing is certain. We do not in fact know that there are not individual works, buried and forgotten, or new and passed over, that have their aesthetic meaning for one person only, or for a minimal audience. They are not, for that reason, without validity. In life itself, in persons, in character, the idiosyncratic is true; the eccentric is true, and valid as eccentric. But just as we can only observe this externally, without feeling it in our bones, so the perfectly private literary work is incommunicable to others. For this reason, whether the private is valid or not, only public works are the ones we can talk about to each other. And in fact all the activity of criticism, written and spoken, is silently based on this assumption. There simply must be norms of some sort, operative at least for large social groups and given historical conditions.

From these considerations it becomes clear that what we most need is a restatement of the relation between a universal consensus and a taste founded in personal differences, taking both of them to be valid notions in spite of apparent contradiction. The one maintains its attractions as an ideal demand, the only thing that can save us socially from total chaos or anarchy of judgement; the other asserts insistently its reality, so that to reject it amounts to wilful obtuseness. Simply accepting a vague, laxly permissive idea of relativism is no solution of the problem. I propose to base such a restatement not on general grounds of what criticism is, or ought to be, but on a view that distinguishes two *functions* for literature. On the one hand, we can distinguish a public and social function, in the sense that literature enshrines a vast total of thought, feeling, and experience gathered through the centuries since literary creation began and which is available in a certain measure, partially rather than completely, to everyone; and on the other hand, an individual, personal, function, because it can be selectively treated by individuals and assimilated to the process of their own thought, sensibility, and spiritual character. In my view this happens continuously as a reality of reading and thinking. Concentrating too much on the logical problem of what criticism is, or ought to be and do, people lose sight of the question as to what literature itself does—how it exists in people's minds and affects their being. Losing this is to lose a good part of what literature is and means. You cannot normalize literary works for the dream of an average reader; idiosyncrasy is at work on both sides, in author and reader, all the time. Hence the following attempt to find an answer to the difficult problem of legitimate variation of taste and judgement in the idea of a double function of literature.

2

DIFFERENT ATTITUDES TO LITERATURE: AFFINITY AND CURIOSITY

THE sort of problem I have in mind belongs perhaps to philosophy of art rather than to aesthetics. The latter concentrates on isolating the principle or feature which makes art, and beauty in art, what they are; differentiating them from other things. But one of the major difficulties of art, especially if you include poetry and literature, has always been that it appears in so many contexts and relationships, including numerous contexts of use. In the thirties R. G. Collingwood, in his *Principles of Art*, dealt with this problem brilliantly by following up one discussion after another on the lines of 'art is not . . .'— not magic, not craft, not ritual, not entertainment, and so on. This had the merit of being extremely logical; you were going straight to the point, discovering the feature in art that was specific and individual, making art into something different from all these other things. However, although this is in fact what most writers on aesthetics try to do, precisely because it is logical, it might be very natural to adopt the opposite point of view; to say, in short, that since art is so often mixed up with other things, then its nature can only be defined by including in some way these other things. A parallel case could be that of soil. You can dig up and analyse a handful of earth, but that would not suffice to form a good enough conception of soil. What happens with and through soil, the fact that there is an interchange with the atmosphere and that things grow out of it, belongs to the conception of what soil is and does. Similarly, it is in the very nature of art not to be susceptible of total isolation. When it *is* isolated you slither over into the area of 'the aesthete', and 'aestheticism', which are terms carrying derogatory meanings. The variety of aesthetic theories derives to some extent from the fact that one or another feature can be isolated and used as the central pivot of a theory; mimesis, expression, symbolism, formalism, intuitionalism, the semiotic, are all used in this way. But literature and art are, and do, several things simultaneously. They are a mode of knowledge, external or internal, affective, psychological; they are representation, and varyingly symbolic; they are play and exuberance, a mode of spiritual freedom or ecstasy; they are, applied to experience, a criticism of life, a medium of evaluation, implicit as in drama or fiction, or explicit as in comedy and satire; they are a kind of ritual, instrumental to belief, as we shall especially note later. The list is not exhausted. It is this multivalency that we are concerned with in this chapter.

One of the advantages of pursuing a philosophy of art instead of an aesthetic is that your field of inquiry is more comprehensive; it can take as its subject both the nature of art, or of different kinds of art, and also the association of art with use of various kinds, and, developing this further, the function of art in the life of the individual and of social groups.

With this in mind let us forget for a moment the common view that good literature is there before us and what we have to do is quickly and steadily to read as much of it as possible, and learn to appreciate it. Because another view is possible. If we scrutinize our habits, we find we that really have two attitudes towards literature. We are naturally interested in exploring a great deal of it; but we are extremely sensitive to the works and authors and kinds that please us particularly and that we want to keep with us and read repeatedly.

Here we must interpose a comment on the ideal or imaginal character of literary works. Thinking first of the whole corpus of literature, we remember that all works are idea; they are in an important sense a-historical. They may possibly derive from experience, sensations, and thought, but in themselves they are a formula, a result, and bear some resemblance as such to other statements of ideas, scientific laws, or philosophical theory. They belong to the collection of statements that are time-less, independent of living-time. They become a part of the general memory, of the general mind. They cannot be altered; they can only be interpreted and, over very long periods of time, become possibly less comprehensible. Hence their a-historical character is not the same thing as present potency, or vital relevance. All works, like all ideas, are co-present to the mind as ideas, whatever their origin, but not as *forces* with effect.

We must also remember, especially in face of the enormous seriousness with which we institutionalize literature and its propagation in research and education, that we mostly accept, explicitly or implicitly, a very important assumption about the imagination. It is that this faculty, operating intensively as in genius, effects a revelation; that it mediates between our knowledge and spiritual values; that it brings into view something far transcending the common-sense or practical consciousness, enabling us to enter a state of vision. With this idea we touch the plane of a quite supra-personal order and understanding. Genius, in this operation, is no more than a medium; its statements are not personal ones. Poetry, literature, art appear then not as the sum of *x* personal statements; they show a supra-personal order seen through the medium of the imagination as a human, but not a personal, faculty. Literature is then not the speech of men, but is projected as by a universal voice; its statements confront one almost as though they existed with a supernatural intactness, not issuing from, but only overheard by human mind. This has to be seen, however, in relation to the other aspect of much literature, which is the aspect of expression, of expressive personal statement. We must remember, too, that this supra-personal functioning of the imagination cannot altogether escape the conditions of personal style within which it has to work; the greatest poets, the greatest imaginations still have an individual style. Both these aspects belong to the nature and functioning of literature. The visionary, and the expressive, are complementary kinds or aspects of literature, not to be confused, nor judged in the same way.

With this in mind and thinking of the whole corpus of literature we can assume that every reader has, in a very general way, a good deal of appreciation of the collectively established canon. But I should like to distinguish grades of understanding. For each of us there is an outer ring of works, of which, though they may well be distant from oneself, one can acknowledge the power, the fact of their belonging to poetic creation; but one may not be able to respond to them with any great warmth. There is, next, a middle belt of works for which one has an understanding that is enlivened with discrimination and a good deal of response, though one may find one's judgement being exercised in a cool, considered way, with some positive and some negative elements; in short, with fair but nevertheless partial appreciation. Finally, however, there is the inner ring, the pieces that we choose, or that choose themselves, because of some intuitive sympathy, some correspondence between them and either our nature, or our present needs, or phase of development, and which make the personal canon within the public canon. We become rapidly skilled in gauging the special attractiveness of works selected in this way.

Thus we are aware that there are many pieces of literature which we are content to become acquainted with and then forget, or at least keep only in the background of memory; and then within that field we recognize a smaller area which becomes a preserve of our own, rather as though it were our property, or an extension of ourselves.

Now these two areas stand for quite different things in our mental existence. Taking the latter first we note how it is related intimately to ourselves; it has a particular affinity with our character, mentality, sensibility, and intellectual constitution. For this reason we assimilate it easily and make it part of ourselves. The factors dominating such a relationship with an intuitively selected part of literature are sympathy and affinity. And this literature of affinity tends to become a corpus that not only exists as aesthetic object confronting us, but also draws us into a context of active influence. The works here involved provide the basis for an effect analogous to that of rituals. Here we feel 'power' and 'relevance'.[1]

---

[1] The following remarks by John Holloway are relevant: 'They have taught us to see myths as activities of story telling, activities that feed and sustain the fabric of primitive society by supplying it with the energy the myths generate in their telling. Rudolf Otto, in the idea of the holy, has taught us to think of holiness as not the holding of theological and moral doctrines, but a complex and decisive *experience* going beyond and below morality, momentous because it puts us in contact with what seems like a great source of superhuman energy and power. A generation has passed since these men were writing. It is time that criticism caught up. Instead, frightened by "art for art's sake", we have so far been discussing poetry on the basis of a paradigm which is ultimately that not of imaginative literature, but of discursive writing and argument. Instead, we must turn from static to dynamic; from the answers that the work is thought to make, to the power it generates through its movement forwards. In brief, from thinking of the poem as embodied doctrine, to thinking of it as embodied energy. Not, in short, meaning: but art. A work of art is an event before it is a meaning: as also it is power, before it is beauty.' John Holloway, *The Colours of Clarity* (London, 1964), pp. 143–4.

The motive, on the other hand, dominating our relationship with the larger field, the whole extent of literature, is curiosity, and the willingness to accept *partial* enjoyment or understanding. It is a curiosity both aesthetic and philosophical, and it is the complementary force to that of sympathy. Neither is inferior to the other as an initial impulse. They operate concurrently, but they divide the literature we read into two sections with different meanings. It is rather like the distinction in the self; we are one self, not two, but we comprehend a social and an intimate self, which are complementary, the one self in different aspects.

Another way of putting this would be to say that literature has two main uses; first, as an element in one's personal life, so that it acquires a ritualistic colouring in association with beliefs and values. It belongs to a process of self-constitution, in the interests of which works are 'used' to implement a *credo*, felt beliefs, or a style of thought and life, because they are symbolic or expressive of these things and have ritualistic, creating, and confirming power. The other use derives from its being a vast repository of the ideas, emotions, experience, and spirituality of all mankind, amidst which one moves in a process of discovery and experimentation, in the widest space of ideas and sensibility. Under this aspect it may be said to mediate principally forms of truth, or to embody symbolically the most highly *generalized* human feelings (love, grief, aspiration, etc.). Literature sometimes functions in one way for us, sometimes in the other. This means that the pattern of reaction is not the same for all the works we read; we do not undergo, or assimilate ourselves to, a single structure of aesthetic experience of unvarying type. As readers we lead two lives all the time. Under one aspect we see literature as a complete and permanent sum of works, which, if we are widely read and studious, we observe and analyse, and organize for ourselves into ordered patterns from various points of view, changing the patterns, moreover, playing with them, moving the pieces about. Under the other aspect we yield to the forces of affinity, living a reader's life of intuitive sympathies, along a curve of personal determination. These two areas of literature do not necessarily remain unchanged as one's life and reading develop. They are collaborative forces; the search for the sympathetic makes one curious, whilst curiosity can lead one to extend the area of the sympathetic. For though we speak of confirming our own nature, our own self, we do not conceive this self as narrow, restricted, and easily circumscribed. It is contained by its own form against the rest of the world, but it has its depths and spaces, which are discovered over a lifetime. It grows, changes, develops, even whilst keeping a predominant identity. As this self experiences literature it is exposed in consequence to a continuous dialectical relationship of the two areas designated by the literature of affinity and that of curiosity. I repeat, we are not dividing literature into two kinds; we are suggesting that it divides for the individual according to its functions for his aesthetic and humanist curiosity on the one hand and the passionate commitment of his taste on the other. On the impulse of curiosity the self reaches constantly into the world beyond itself in order to assimilate and to grow. Thus authors and works that at an earlier stage are thought not to be germane to the self may later become so, and then be translated into the area of the sympathetic, finding a place in a mutation of the personal ritual. The search for the self and the search for truth, intuitive and rational understanding intertwined, progress side by side.

This is not quite what C. S. Lewis refers to in speaking of the reasons why we read. His answer to this question is that we seek 'an enlargement of our being', that we try to see other perspectives than our own. The idea is interesting and seems to be near to the point of view I am putting forward, if left in the most general terms. But his closer definition takes him further away, because his idea, influenced no doubt by his religious views, is that literature is a way by which we can escape from our self into another; it is a way of overcoming self-love and entering into a perfect humanity. The spirit of my argument is more secular, though the process I seek to indicate is not less mysterious. Self-transcendence belongs to it; in the sense, however, of breaking through the limitations of an undeveloped self and continually extending it, continually unfolding its spiritual powers. This might ultimately be linked with the creativity inhering in life generally, here apprehended in the process of self-identification and self-affirmation. My present argument is, however, restricted to clarifying the relation of personal taste to the available stock of canonized literature.

I think that two species, or at least two strains or tendencies, of criticism arise in relation to these two experiences of literature. They exist in most critics and readers, and they are complementary, but differently motivated and energized. The one is criticism-as-interpretation. It is under the impulsion of sympathy and affinity that the finest kinds of this are produced, giving studies that on the basis of consanguinity penetrate most deeply into their subject. They flow from choice, from intimate knowledge, and, so long as they are controlled by judgement and not spoiled by undiscriminating enthusiasm, they are the most positive and rewarding contributions to the criticism of understanding and exegesis. This strain of criticism comes to the fore whenever a critic is in the closest rapport with his author. The other kind arises in us in relation to both canonized literature, the corpus of historical works declared by the common voice to be worthy of study, and also to new works. In these areas curiosity dominates, and the motivation of criticism is far more complex, since there is enormous variety. Many works, and aspects of works, many authors, and parts of authors, may appear partly acceptable and partly problematic to the keen-thinking reader. This kind of criticism includes a measure of assent, but it also constitutes the endless assault, or partial assault, launched by innumerable disagreements and dissatisfactions which originate in philosophical or temperamental diversity. Here a vast, unquenchable, unceasing debate comes into operation; it is the endless discussion and re-discussion of *all* the ideas, beliefs, feelings, symbols, and values that may be involved and are differently viewed by different individuals, and different cultural groups, or by the same individual at different times. These two kinds, the criticism of affinity and that of debate, are complementary, as are the literature of committed taste and that of curiosity.

We are here making a distinction in the motivation of criticism, which is not the same thing as differences in critical method. Methods are often discussed, but motivation has not to my knowledge been much examined. So at a later stage some problems connected with it will be looked at. First, however, it is convenient to follow up questions raised by the functions of literature.

3

FUNCTIONS AND USES OF
LITERATURE

AT the outset let it be said that 'the function' of literature is not
the same thing as its having a variety of functions and uses.
Speaking in the singular we can say quite simply that literature,
like other arts, fulfils the natural function of satisfying natural
aesthetic needs. But in discussing a literature of affinity, and the
personal canon we make for ourselves, we observed that literature under this aspect cannot be confined within the fashionable notion of the 'aesthetic object'; it has an energy that affects
the reader more directly. The purist conception of aesthetic
experience gives way here to the sense of something functional,
and the question of the 'uses' of literature arises. What are the
uses of literature, and in what way can they be legitimately
defended in relation to purely aesthetic values? And how do
they affect criticism?

It will be obvious that too-simple ideas of use will be out of
place in this context. As we follow the problem of affinity, and
the conditions of individualized taste, we shall be aware constantly of different uses, of uses both direct and indirect, and
sometimes of disunity as well as unity, in the pattern of function
within the relationship of a reader to a work. By direct uses I
mean here the obvious application of literature seen in religious
poetry and plays, in all direct moralizing stories, in social
parables, and in propaganda literature, social or political. With
these I am at the moment less concerned, though they will each
be discussed at later stages, in more than one connection. By
indirect use I mean the more devious, oblique, or secondary
functions of literature in the psychological continuum of the
individual. For instance, one of the more straightforward
functions ascribed to art and literature under this head is its
therapeutic value. It could be looked on as a sophisticated,
modern elaboration of the idea of catharsis, a very long-term
insight of Aristotle and one enlarged upon at an early stage of

modern times by Goethe. I. A. Richards's theory of the balancing and harmonizing of impulses belongs to this direction of
thought, as do the theories of Adrian Stokes, worked out in a
more precisely clinical framework, and deriving as they do from
Melanie Klein's psychology.

But it is also important to note, in these introductory observations, that there is often a criss-cross of value reactions and
therefore of functions. T. S. Eliot, for instance, because of his
religious themes and ideas, and his deliberate use of contemporary characters and settings in his plays, and, furthermore, because of his search for a discreet poetic diction for drama, may
well cause very disharmonious reactions in his readers, and it
might be difficult to pin down the value responses as of aesthetic
or non-aesthetic origin. A reader might not, for instance, be very
interested in the specifically Christian foundation of the plot and
ideas of *The Elder Statesman*, but he might find the achievement
of a dramatic diction and style impressive, and the character of
the style to his taste. But again, although style is apparently a
matter of form, the values admired in the style might not be
purely aesthetic, in the sense of being values inhering only in
art-works. It is a very clean, precise style; it has attractive,
quiet, conversational tones, and flexibility, but is never lax; it is
firm, and luminous when touching the emotions. There is
discretion in it; it is cool, chaste, urbane. Such qualities are not
confined to art objects; some of them are sensuous, and therefore aesthetic, but others more intellectual or abstract, and such
as appear in things outside art; in persons, for example, or in
actions. This indicates what I mean by a criss-cross of value
reactions; it is not a question of rejecting the Christian subject
and ideas, and accepting the style, the aesthetic values (i.e. of
admiring the work not for its content but 'as art', 'as literature').
It is a much more complex pattern of acceptance and rejection,
taste and distaste, agreement and disagreement, harmony and
discord, in respect of all the various factors of subject and
expression in the work and its ambience. Let us note, however,
that if some factors in a work run counter to a person's taste or
interests, that work ceases, to that extent, to *function*, as an art-
work, for that person. Its impact, effect, influence are reduced;
it does less for one. What is involved here is taste, and value
response, not a logic of critical criteria or standards. We see how

use or function is absolutely relevant to art, in strict contrast to rational or scientific knowledge which is independent of complex personal contexts. Literary criticism, which has to analyse and adjust to such mixed phenomena and contexts, is correspondingly complex, shifting, and fluid.

In recent times the main inquiry has not been directed to these aspects of literature and art, because interest centred on their purely aesthetic nature. The guiding belief of critics for the last three or four decades has been in a posited autonomy of art and the art-work. The idea that art could be used has been anathema, and the mere suggestion of it like a red rag to a bull. The general direction has been to isolate the verbal aesthetic object. It was not argued *whether* it could be isolated, but it was asserted that it must be, since aesthetic experience as something *per se* was posited and pre-supposed. Of course, the literature of commitment, especially in its aggressive forms in political and ideological writing, extending often even to lyric poetry, ran counter to the autonomy view, but its excessive and all too obvious partisan content had the effect, not of drawing attention, as it might easily have done, to a legitimate function for art, but of emphasizing the charms of detachment and virginal autonomy.

The historical background to this in England is the Victorian and Edwardian view of literature as an instrument of knowledge and wisdom, with the function of edification. The power to edify was the commonest criterion. But edification was a blinkered conception, being interpreted on the lines of the narrow kinds of Victorian morality. It was the degree to which literature had been subjugated to this that really set off the alarm in the 1920s and brought a very strong reaction. But in the purist rebound all notions of function or use were thrown into the same rag-bag as conventional moral didacticism, and the theoretical aesthetic object was put on the pedestal vacated by edification. An error was at work in all this, which can be expressed by saying that the aesthetic *integrity* of a work does not necessarily, as was thought, contradict the notion of the work's having functions or uses. A hymn tune or cantata has musical integrity but also a use in the church service, and it cannot be said either that the use disrupts or degrades the integrity, or that the two aspects are independent. The position to be adopted in this chapter is that all works have aesthetic character and give an aesthetic experience but may also, simultaneously, fulfil a function, or several, for the individual reader. Applicability, or usability, is not a particular criterion of aesthetic value in the narrow sense; but any work may be assimilated into a mind, a sensibility, and their activity, into a spiritual or philosophical process of being, without offending its aesthetic integrity. To take a very simple analogy, you could have a simple rectangular building, or an elegant, well-proportioned room, which need not be designed functionally, in the sophisticated architectural sense, but which could function in various ways and serve various purposes. It could be a meeting place, a one-room dwelling, a workshop or studio, a schoolroom, and so on. As a building or a room it is usable in any case. But none of these uses or functions is a criterion of its being a good building or a well-proportioned room. Its usability or functional character is thus part of its being a building or a room without being an aesthetic criterion. Similarly with literature; it is a mistake to try to negate the natural ambience or functional contexts of a literary work on the basis of a rigid notion of aesthetic autonomy.[1]

[1] The point was touched upon in a clear statement by Sidney Zink: 'But I think that we can react to a work of art as art, and also give it other uses in other parts of experience. In its own nature any work of art is a self-contained individual, and to experience it in its proper nature is to experience it as an integral, self-subsistent whole. But this self-contained experience is itself a member of a varied field of experience, and the recognition of the autonomy of art as art should not obscure the relations of art to other things. Let us insist first, as Croce does, that although art incorporates into itself materials from the rest of life, it incorporates them completely, in such a way that these materials acquire a new nature and meaning, independent of their actual sources and potential references. But we should recognise, second, that this independence which the aesthetic experience insistently asserts is as insistently repudiated by the larger body of experience to which it belongs. In short, life will not allow art to exist merely as art. Men try to organise their lives and to see the bearing of their experience and kinds of experience on one another. The experience of art occurs in a field of experience; and, although it may try to plant its flag on a particular corner of that field, to assert its absolute autonomy and prohibit intercourse with the others, it cannot prevent its neighbours from clustering about its borders, and, if not making military invasions, at least paying visits as interested tourists. A man may be intensely interested in art, and care for nothing but the particular and isolated apprehensions of individuality which each work of art provides. But most persons who are seriously interested in art will also be seriously interested in the other spheres of life, and the force of interest in these separately will also be a force of interest in their relations. A man interested in painting and in history would be a strangely segmented creature who was not also interested in the history of painting and of the influence of painting in history.

The literature of affinity, as I have called the individual's chosen canon, is closely connected with the idea of use or function. In the following pages I shall assume that affinity, or special sympathy with an author or work, presupposes the likelihood of uses for such work.

Taking first the larger question of subject and ideas, their much neglected importance appears with complete freshness when reconsidered in the light of the several and varied functions of literature. For personal taste and the personal use of literature they are relevant at the sophisticated level, not merely at the naive one. Everything concerning subject, materials, and ideas in a work includes interests and values that stretch from the simpler levels of sensuous reaction to the complicated ones of intellectual, emotional, and moral character; and all these vary from individual to individual in patterns of great complexity, making taste partly subjective and variable, and in consequence giving the basis for the relativist position in criticism. The outcry against the subject in art in the second and third decades of this century, with critics like Fry and Bell, was based, like that against use, either on a misunderstanding, or on partisan overstatement of a new point of view. It arose from the reaction against a realism that had become pedestrian; against the implication that realistic representation of objects, for the sake of illusion, was the purpose of art; and it was a defence of new non-figurative styles. The corollary of this view would be, and indeed was often taken to be, that any artist or poet could treat any subject; which is untrue. Authors and artists write and paint not about just anything lying around, but about themes and subject-matter that hold a particular interest for them, as the cause either of conflicts or problems, or deep emotional or philosophical reactions. They are in this respect in thrall to forces outside their control, and whether they are what used to be called objective or subjective in style has no importance for this point. Even Shakespeare, reputed to be the most objective of writers, was not an absolute god of creation; he had his range and kind of subjects, as Dante, Donne, and Wordsworth theirs. Writers are aware of the factitious work they produce when they are not really engaged by the subject. Subject always matters, just as beliefs do.

But again we must recognize the inclusive situation without making false deductions about criteria. Neither the subject nor a belief make a poem a poem, but in a poem which involves them they are important elements in *that* poem; they are part of the total expression. In a poem the poet gives more than just belief; he represents belief as a factor in a context of experience. Belief, in a poem, is belief plus the poet, belief together with the poet's coming to, or holding, that belief, with his way of believing. A poem is a representation that *includes* the belief. To a reader who is in sympathy with an author's belief or subject, his poem or work means more; not as bare belief, but as poem including the belief. People who read religious poetry must be supposed to want both religion and poetry, not one or the other. They want religion *in the poem*, desirous of satisfying two sides of their nature at once, in an agreeable and rich harmony. All this applies equally to the religious poetry of, for example, Herbert, or to the implicit rationalism of Pope, or to the pantheism of romantic poets; but also to sceptics, who like not merely pure poetry but poetry impregnated with the values of scepticism.

It seems to me that T. S. Eliot's position on this problem was as reasonable as any. He believed in his religious ideas; he used them in his poetry; but he did not write poetry for the purpose of propagating them. This allows both for the fact that a subject-matter and ideas are important to the author, and to the poem, without being a didactic reason for the poem's existence. It avoids the error in so much argument on this issue of wishing to reduce the status, either of the poetry, or of the ideas, to one of subordination.[1] For works of imaginative literature, like works of art, have their several aspects which combine in different ways. To these belong both the cognitive and the expressive. Beyond that, they are also affirmations, either wholly or in part. They are not only static, self-contained, still, smiling objects in an emptied space. They derive often from the power of belief, and they radiate that power. As mimesis or representation they show things; as expression they provide an

[1] Cf. T. S. Eliot, *The Use of Poetry and the Use of Criticism* (London, 1933), p. 136. Eliot's arguments do, however, leave a loop-hole for associating the strictly poetic simply with emotion and feeling, which in my view is too narrow.

outlet for violent emotion or conflict; but they exist also as a kind of superlative declaration; they affirm attitudes and responses to life and the world; they project creeds, values, and deep responses to destiny, the conquest of suffering, and the pursuit of harmony.

This dynamic aspect of art and poetic works only seems to conflict with aesthetic integrity. In fact the relation between them is real and harmonious, though extremely subtle. In their affirmative or assertive qualities lie their potential 'uses' in the spiritual processes and self-assertion of the reader. But their meaning must be established and secure before they can function. The art-work encases the meaning in its so-called integrity. Because of this integrity, which is objective, unassailable, the same for all readers, the work can have a function, as an affirmation, for *some*. Otherwise, the affirmation would be a form of personal *behaviour*, both in the author and in the reader; it would be physical action, not spiritual process. Thus function does not detract from integrity, as is often thought, nor integrity exclude function; on the contrary, they are interdependent and in balance.

There has been extensive dissension in the critical attitudes of recent decades on this problem of subject, thought, politico-moral implications, and aesthetic values in their interrelatedness in literary works. Take the following passage from Sutton's *Modern American Criticism* (pp. 105–6):

> To those who are not orthodox Christians but who are interested in the innumerable ways in which literature treats values, Eliot's pronouncement may seem confining. Most of our 'greatest' Western literature derives power and interest from the ways in which it reacts against orthodoxy and generally accepted conventions. If a 'common agreement on ethical and theological matters' could be achieved, there would be little occasion for literature as a free enquiry into the conditions of human life.

This passage illustrates a very commonly held view. It is indeed the basis of a vast amount of present-day criticism, and the approach to literature altogether. But it rests on an unproved assumption: for who laid down that literature should be the occasion of a 'free inquiry' into the conditions of human life? It may be this, of course, for agnostics, sceptics, freethinkers, and liberal moralists; this is a post-eighteenth-century development.[1] But they are not the only people interested in literature, and not the only ones who inquire into the conditions of human life; theologians, philosophers, moralists, sociologists, do this. Scepticism is not a prerequisite of literary interest. Or take this passage, which illustrates a common way of arguing:

No matter what he takes his function to be, the validity of the critic's analysis depends on the validity of the *aesthetic* judgement that he must make. For even if he should not be interested in pure aesthetic values, but should seek to discover the relation of the art object under analysis to other interests, he cannot discriminate with clarity the relationship between art and anything else—whether it be politics or morality or religion or science—unless he has a clear knowledge of the value as art of the object whose relationship he is seeking to disclose. (Eliseo Vivas, *Creation and Discovery* (New York, 1955), p. 193.)

The argument here is circular because it presupposes an art-object 'with a relationship' to other 'interests', instead of facing the fact that the other interests are built into the art-object, are internal elements of it, not external relational objects. *Partage de Midi*, or *Le Soulier de Satin*, or Eliot's plays, do not 'have a relationship with' religion; it is built in. The argument is also quite sterile. Take, for instance, the form of the fable, and consider La Fontaine. If the art applied to composing a fable makes it clearer, then it is a better *fable*. The moral point is not neutralized by an aesthetic object but sharpened into a work of art called a fable. If, on the other hand, the moral were a bad or vulnerable one the aesthetic object would lose its meaning and importance. No fables illustrate bad morals. The problem in all this is not that non-literary elements (religion, morals etc.) prevent or distort an aesthetic judgement; it is that they *complete* understanding; that without them judgement is impossible. In short, not their consideration, but their non-consideration, distorts criticism.

My present argument about works of literature having a function linked with personal taste is not, however, narrowly concerned with the morality of art or the moral use of literature in the older sense, though these do call for some comments. I think this is what many modern critics have been so afraid of;

---

[1] Cf. the observations of Sartre, in *What is Literature?*, about the way in which under social influences literature in the eighteenth century became centred on doubt, criticism, and the *prise de conscience*.

they rejected the notion, beloved of the Victorian spirit, of an approved literature. But in their violently reactionary desire to pinpoint the aesthetic value as against the moral didacticism they have not been sufficiently clear about the aesthetic itself. They have merely presupposed that a work could in fact be purely aesthetic. How often the phrase occurs: 'but if we consider the book "purely as a novel", or "purely as art" '! What is meant by such phrases? They can only mean, it seems to me, that the philosophy, or political, or moral, ideas of a novel or play should be discounted for this exercise, and the work looked at purely as a mimesis, or an expression (of feelings, mood, etc.); in other words, as a vehicle of truth, or a pretext for vicarious emotions; unless the notion is restricted still further simply to the quality of the verse or prose as craftsman-ship, as texture, as instrument, or technique; which reduces itself to style and vivid expression, sensuous power, *le mot juste*, and figures of speech. Another idea frequently put forward (by Cleanth Brooks, for instance) is that the aesthetic is nothing more nor less, even in lyric poetry, than the presentation of the subject-matter or experience or ideas in their dramatic aspect, which makes the result different from discourse. But this, surely, must end up with a type of formalism; the subject is presented in dramatic form, and is therefore aesthetic. But even if the subject-matter is stripped of 'ideas' we must still remember that every mimesis, every expression, involves some perceptual knowledge or some psychology; in other words, something non-aesthetic. You do not need moral or religious didacticism to create the problem of the importance of subject-matter, and ideas falsely called extra-aesthetic. The subject, and the *Welt-anschauung*, and any ideas, are part of the work, part of it *qua* mimesis or expression; they influence its impact on any given reader, they condition judgement and taste, and they help to determine the uses of this particular piece of literature. Only extreme symbolism gives extreme abstraction of aesthetic quality, and it is then probably beyond interpretation or understanding.[1]

[1] Though I have worked independently there is some coincidence between some ideas here put forward and those of H. D. Aiken in his article 'The Aesthetic Relevance of Belief' (reprinted in *Aesthetic Inquiry: Essays on Art Criticism and the Philosophy of Art*, ed. M. C. Beardsley and H. M. Schueller (Belmont, Calif., 1967), pp. 141–54).

Another modern attitude might usefully be mentioned at this point for its bearing on the question of 'content' and extra-poetic references. Large numbers of critics and scholars work nowadays on the basis that literature is a kind of knowledge, providing insights about life, and particularly about 'the age', that cannot be obtained from any other source. This sort of criticism often starts with literary works and then widens its scope, becoming cultural criticism. It is essentially an analysis of evidence. Writers are taken to be people of seismographic gifts. They register things—impressions, perceptions, feelings, reactions, mental states, fears, desires; and if you look at a largish number of writers in a given period you will be able to make a generalized or typical picture of the look of man and society in it. This is not the same as straightforward social documentation, but it is certainly spiritual documentation.

A good deal of modern American criticism, agnostic and secular in outlook as it is, rests on the spoken or unspoken assumption that literature yields 'the image of man'. And as modern literature itself has thrown off most doctrinal or ortho-dox shackles, or, in other words, lost its functional place in an organic culture, or in an essentially harmonious unity of civilizing forces in society, this yield of an image, of modern man, the modern age, or modern society, became ever more important; for one might well ask, if literature does not at least give this, what else can it stand for at all?

Literature down to the eighteenth century contained always a considerable degree of thought, or was linked to a firm philosophical framework, and it would be an error to say that the fine statement of particular philosophical or moral ideas was only an accidental accompaniment of purely aesthetic or poetic forms. These things were a value which was looked for in literature. After the romantics and their particular form of idealism literature became to a very considerable extent at-tached to social themes, history, contemporary life, and the sciences, as they developed from the earlier nineteenth century onwards. In consequence a new ideal for writing arose, which was that of truth; literature became a truth literature and to a very considerable extent has remained so ever since, consciously. Social documentation, increasing psychological analysis and introspection, realist and naturalist styles, asserted a profound and long-term domination; and the subsequent evolution of expressionist, imagist, and abstract styles may be viewed, in the long perspective, as the production of mechanisms for showing human truth rather than creeds in the old sense of orthodoxies. This is what makes Strindberg now appear as an ancestor of more than one twentieth-century trend, touching as he does all three aspects, social, psychological, and stylistic; and in the latter point, too, providing 'expressionist' fruits after 'naturalist' beginnings. His dialogues embodying the vicious hate relationships between men and women, enacted within a framework of a dominant social morality, are an example of truth literature. Beauty, or aesthetic pleasure, are spectres at the rites of these grim, harrowing subjects; one scarcely goes to them for entertainment, so-called, unless one is perverse in a strict sense. The justification of plays like *The Father* or *The Dance of Death* is that their author, by a combination of experience and imagination, knew a great deal about such relationships and was able to depict their complexity with devastating clarity and truth. This is their value.

By contrast, the so-called decadents, even a man like Wilde, still belong to the idealist kind of writer generated in the romantic period. They still had the sense of communicating a vision; of presenting through literature something that contains the values of aspiring thought, meditation, dream, or the visionary. They are really the last representatives of the secular literary tradition aiming high in this way, and indeed forming high things. They appear in the sharpest contrast to the new truth literature of the nineties so evident in psychological and social theory themes in the drama and in certain areas of the novel.

What appears here is an eager interest, in the spirit of an intensified secularism, in the conditions of life and living. As far as art and literature are concerned, it shows an intense desire to know all about life, to know the best and the worst within the limits of human experience, either in individual or in social forms, and with an increasing sense both of helplessness and of responsibility. The whole development, and a literary criticism growing out of it, is especially apparent in the basic positions of some American critics. Allen Tate is one who believes in 'the image of modern man' as the product of literature; the phrase is one he uses. R. P. Blackmur, too, considers that in the twentieth century art and literature have to carry the whole burden of spiritual values, which, however, is a burden of doubt and exploration rather than of accepted dogma. Lionel Trilling has described how he has lectured on a group of characteristically modern (i.e. earlier twentieth-century) authors and the 'abyss' of truth about modern man that they have revealed. What has been happening here is very significant; because if you combine the idea that art is a thing, an image, *sui generis*, having its own aesthetic integrity, with the fact that it is giving you an image, not of beauty, but of a horrible and terrifying abyss (modern man), then immediately the question arises as to the essential value of looking at an abyss. The images of art formerly gave a view of beauty, or, if their subject-matter was disturbing, a moral was drawn or implied, or the horror of the subject redeemed by a philosophy, as in Dante's Hell, or *Paradise. Lost*, or Shakespearian tragedy. With modern, beliefless literature, and its impact, the requirement of art without dogma rules out a plain moral lesson, even if this has not been made impossible anyhow by a general loss of stateable moral values. So a position is reached where the value of such negative literature must lie in one of two things; either in its giving satisfaction to people who enjoy looking at horror and abysses, in other words perverse pleasure, or in its being simply truth. But even here, in my view, this simple truth-value, where negatives are involved, is an inadequate motivation for the reader. No depressive, negative literature, in the simple state of truthful image, holds readers for long, nor can one maintain permanently and exclusively attitudes of self-abasement. So I come to the conclusion that the positive acceptance of modern abyss-literature is motivated not by the straight desire for truth, as a scientist might desire it, but by the moral belief that to know the truth, bad though it may be, is an obligation on the human condition. You have to have a strong motive to look on horror. And, after all, the sense of the abyss derives from moral discrimination.

In consequence a paradox of all this literature and criticism is clear; for what we are really faced with is not disappearance, but mutation, of the moral factor in assessing the significance of literature. For Arnold and other Victorians the moral judgement was brought directly into play in aesthetic evaluations; a literature that was not in some way elevating (to use one of the recurring notions) was debased, and therefore to be rejected. For the moderns under consideration the aesthetic acceptance of the terrifying but honest image of the dark aspects of life and humanity, presented as suffering and helplessness without compensating consolations, rests on the prior belief that one should in conscience pursue the truth, whatever it is, and whatever it shows. This gives back to literature, even in the areas where it seems to be disclaimed, a functional role and importance, because there is implied in the whole situation the idea of *regeneration*; both individual and society are to be redeemed by the instrument of truth.

A related aspect of literature is that, as a corpus of fiction, of particular stories acting as a vehicle of general human truth, it embodies a vicarious remorse for the guilt of life. Fiction and drama are certainly read for pleasure. But one of the ways in which they become serious is when they are statements of the hidden truth about ourselves. Remorseless statements, to induce remorse. Hidden truths, because we conceal ourselves all the time in our daily affairs. To be plain and outspoken, either about one's private self, or about other private selves, is not discreet, not politic, not judicious or practical, not fair or nice. But somewhere, such is the pressure from one side of human feeling, the truths must be released from privacy and concealment; they must be spoken out, but in a form where the speaking out does not contravene the idealism or deep charity of the impulse to do so; in a form where they do not hurt persons, but only strike home as general perceptions. The literature of fiction is from this point of view a function of humane desires. It is a universalized declaration of penitence; or it is a cry for help; or, alternatively, an act of stoicism.

We turn now to another important aspect of the main problem of this chapter. The literary *kinds*, subjected in recent decades no less than subject and ideas to much negative scrutiny, also have a quite particular significance in connection with the function of literature and its relation to personal taste. Here sensibility and artistic disposition determine preferences; this mechanism is similar to that governing disposition towards the different arts, though with literature it tends to be obscured because the literary kinds are at least linked by the verbal medium. Yet the use of words, and their links with visual and auditory imagery, varies enormously from one literary kind to another, for which reason it is not surprising to find literary enthusiasts often tending strongly towards a primary taste for one of the kinds, for the novel, the drama, or lyric poetry, and even their sub-divisions.

The fact of different art forms deriving from different gifts means that no art is prescribable. Whether we like it or not, there can be no categorical imperative about the arts. They depend on natural endowment in individuals. This is part of the gratuitous nature of art. But the corollary should be obvious; the *functional* importance of an art for those with the disposition towards it is of great significance. What applies to separate arts applies in my view to some extent also to the literary kinds. The writing of odes, for instance, depends on temperament, or on distinctive period modes of feeling; they were common in the eighteenth and early nineteenth centuries, and are today almost non-existent. Parables, religious or political (Bunyan or Brecht), are the effects and instruments of didactically minded people. Tragedy, comedy, satire, as Hume pointed out, derive from, and give implementation to, particular tastes. Some people take pleasure in all these forms, but most have favourites amongst them. There can be no doubt that the kinds, which for long now have been treated as though, aesthetically, their genre character were irrelevant, are in fact of great significance in connection with the uses of literature. They are usually determined by particular motives, the impulse to praise (hymn), to mock (parody), to teach (fable, parable), and so on, and thus appear naturally in functional contexts. Subject-matter, emotional attitudes, and values are intricately connected in the various genres which represent them and create on that basis communities of readers. I think that in this respect writers, and the majority of readers, think and feel alike. For it is what you are full of, what haunts you, what pushes your thoughts and feelings in certain directions and won't leave go, that determines what you write; and also what readers read with greater, or lesser, interest. The simpler reactions, overlaid in modern education and academic specialization by sophisticated patterns, are the more reliable guide in the problem before us.

Liberating the notion of use or function in this way from simple moral and didactic contexts, we are free to use the idea of ritual, or ritualistic colouring, in a new way. I have said that the literature of personal selection or taste acquires a force analogous to that of ritual. I do not mean by this that poetry is a substitute for ritual or dogma formerly attached to religion, nor do I refer to a ritual connected with myths reconceived in some modern form. I mean that each reader can select a corpus of works which would have the effect of constituting an instrument of faith for him; of *his* faith, *credo*, philosophy of life, set of values; or for his *scepticism*, because the sceptic also makes a choice and supports it. These works, by subject, tenor, and style will correspond to his nature and spiritual complexion, and as he reads and re-reads them he enacts a ritual of his own deepest desires and impulses. Literature taken up in this way is not only truth but implemented truth; it is activated, incorporated into a total act of living, of creating and maintaining the self in its characteristic intellectual and spiritual form and existence. Again, let me emphasize that I am not indicating a specific kind of literary works for this purpose; it is a question of the same works fulfilling, or not fulfilling, a function for different individuals. From the author's point of view, we must acknowledge the essential relevance of meanings in his works to his mind and constitution, and the way he thinks and acts his own life. His works are a kind of deed. They are constitutive, and not simply representational impressions, cognitive of an outside man or nature. They are extensions of himself, just as in a political career a man's projects and achievements are not separate, neutral entities, but projections of himself, part of the dynamics of his living. We acknowledge this in the language we employ to speak of poets. 'Wordsworth' is neither Mr. Wordsworth nor a short-hand sign for 'the works of William Wordsworth'; it is the personality name for Wordsworth and his poems, Wordsworth and what he made, a mind in motion on its living course, self-revealing, like a comet with its energy, its direction, and trail of self-evidence.

From the reader's point of view, the response to certain works and authors with special sympathy is related to the syndrome just described in writers. I make a choice. I select. I pick out the works that feed my taste, my longings and desires. I read them, and repeat the reading; doing that, I rehearse my own nature, I become clear about myself, assert myself, renew myself. It is on a par with any natural activity or self-fulfilment.

It is in this sense that each author, and indeed each work, has his or its circle of readers, the converse of each reader having his circle of authors or works. In this sense there is a public for poetic works on religious themes, on subjects connected with the passions, on social themes, and so on. Every work divides the potential audience into those who are curious, tasting and passing on, and those who respond intimately. The most obvious example for this phenomenon is religious writing, or devotional poetry. The perfect paradigm from orthodoxy is the reading of the Old and New Testaments lesson by lesson in the Church Service through the year in ritual repetition. The formal repetition is alive and mysterious, because the verbal meanings and the rite are one single thing. As Eliot said, when the Bible is seen as poetry only, it will be an aesthetic vacuum, and will cease to be read at all. But the same applies to any philosophy, any set of values forming the basis of living. We do not need an orthodox church for this, nor would that be the norm today, nor would it cover all the aspects of feeling involved. Hölderlin once spoke in a letter of a future in which freedom of thought and philosophy would have increased a thousandfold, so that each individual would have his own 'religion' and celebrate his 'deities' in appropriate, creative rituals. He used the vocabulary of religion to describe his premonition, but it applies by analogy to all systems of beliefs.

It may be argued that this is subjective. So it is; but subjectivity is not equivalent to the eccentric, the absolute private, which is mental isolation or breakdown. The subjective is the inter-subjective; it is something that can be understood by, and shared with, others, though not necessarily *all* others. The point of my argument is that this subjectivity, this individualized imaginative and emotional context or area, is valid precisely *because* it is person-focused. It is in no way, as is often implied in conventional critical writing, aesthetically irrelevant and inferior because it falls short of some incredible universal ideal, or because art, for 'true' judgement, must be impersonal, objective, and in principle available as a compulsory value to all who try hard enough. In the sequel the question of how the personal field of interest and understanding comes to be extended will be discussed. For the moment our purpose is simply to stress the ritualistic function of literature as legitimate and in no way contradictory to its aesthetic character.

We have recounted a part of the evidence leading us to stress again the functional aspects of literature. Varying from individual to individual they are essential to the nature of literary works, as to art in general, and I have tried to show that they do not conflict with the notion of aesthetic integrity; to equate integrity with a rigid idea of autonomy, and with a single type of aesthetic being, is to veil the complex nature and ambience of literary works by a falsely applied, restrictive, deforming logic. It is necessary to restore this balance against three particularly strong paradigms of recent decades. One, already referred to, is the theoretical concentration on the aesthetic object, which in literature is the verbal construct in verse or prose. A second is the pattern of academic study, and the consequent imposition of scholarship and its ideals and methods on the educational transmission of literature, based as it is on the implicit assumption of a catholic taste and an ideally universal standard. A third is the professional critic of the better quality journals, whose job it is to have wide sympathies with literature and its products, the so-called 'world of books', and to be ever at the ready with some piece of fair comment. However this professional job evolved, its fulfilment in present-day conditions makes it certain that the bookworm type, the omnivorous reader, the extremely knowledgeable and quick, agile type of mind will be called to undertake it, and we forget that such minds are but one of many kinds and represent only one type of critical attitude and literary sensibility. The situation now is that with professional scholarship and journalistic alertness we have all the knowledge about all the branches of literature, historical and current, but we forget that these activities are distorting, professional excrescencies on the normal life of literature. They are natural outgrowths, no doubt; I am not saying they are an evil, or should not exist. But in our present cultural and educational climate they appear to be the ministering angels who make literature viable and important, whilst in reality they veil part of its true nature and function. Formerly, or so we should like to imagine, the individual reader knew less about the whole available stock, and more about the branch or kind that his experience and discriminating taste selected as of particular concern for him personally.

The catholic principle is suspect, and the notion of the universal can only be taken in a relative sense, as the not-only-singular, not-only-individual. We must accept as a fact, with logical consequences for reading, taste, and education, that literature is determined by different psychological-expressive motives, to which correspond different uses in the reader; and that to try to accommodate literature—as product and reception—under a single principle of pure aesthetics is to neglect some of its essential aspects. What needs to be invest-igated now is the psychology of art-creation, and literary creation, in all their variety. What are the motives in writing poems and fictions of quite bewilderingly diverse kinds, and what the motives for reading them? Because the difficulty lies in the diversity being real; it is not infinite variation of one motive and one pattern. A game, football, tennis, cricket, is a true variation, in an infinite series, of a single basic pattern, a tight framework of a small number of rules and conventions; and its motive in human psychology is relatively simple. Literature and art are not like that. They vary continuously a large number of patterns that are themselves varied at the start. Their psychological motivation is extremely complex. Aesthet-ics, poetics, and criticism are not like the theory of a game; they are not concerned with things that can be easily traced to a single principle. They are obliged to account for diversity.

Literature is a function of living, except when it is segregated as a hermetic, professional study-object. It is parallel to all living, with infinite plasticity, and shares its complexity as though it were life itself. A consequence of this is that poems and fictions must mean many different things to different people, their function constantly varying. Another consequence is the ease with which diverse philosophies and ideologies—Christian-ity, romanticism, various humanisms, Marxism, scepticism, etc.—provide each their own *theory* of literature; or, as I would rather say, a theory for their *own* literature, the literature of their own taste, linked functionally with it. A vivid example of how one can hive off one branch of literature and speak of it as of literature in the absolute is the beginning of Charles du Bos's *What is Literature?*:[1] 'What is Literature—literature worthy of the name, the only one that concerns us here, and the only one that ever counted for me?' What 'worthy' signifies emerges in the sequel as the author focuses on a mystical, religious kind of poetry, a visionary poetry concerned with questions about last things. Authors are successively evoked who in fact provide an interesting example of a pattern of affinity—Dante, Shelley, Keats; the critic Middleton Murry on Keats; Charles Morgan's *The Fountain*; Stefan George, Emerson, Wordsworth, Longinus, Goethe, Vaughan, in selective and directed quotations. These all bear on the idea du Bos makes his centre, the idea of a 'discourse of the soul', the vehicle of which is poetry. This is a somewhat radical example of a selected 'personal' literature, but its positive character as a literature of affinity with functional significance has to be accepted, in my view. The error in du Bos's position is to argue exclusively that this one kind of literature is the only 'worthy' one.

Other important symptoms of the inclusive situation we envisage—the work plus its ambience, the work as an energy nucleus radiating into a reader-context—are some of the conceptions generated, apparently by criticism but really by literature, in both past and present. Poetry as dream, poetry as myth, poetry as expression, as symbol, as mimesis, literature as parable, as vision, as wisdom, as truth, as fantasy, as 'criticism of life', as confession, as protest, as experiment—what are these common and legitimate indications but pointers to different functions comprehended as essential to the character of works under discussion? They are not mere classification. They suggest a much more vital typology than some traditional ones, or formal categories, and are certainly more energetic than monoform catholic receptivity.

All these factors together show how complex the situation is for the making of judgements, and for the ideally directed attempt to secure some rationalization of agreements and disagreements in criticism. They show that literature is not susceptible of simple isolation as autotelic aesthetic object; this is a

[1] Charles du Bos, *What is Literature?* (London, 1940).

theoretical projection for clarifying one, but not all, of its aspects. We see that literature also operates within a framework of vital, psychological, and cultural values; values, moreover, which are the same in both the aesthetic and the non-aesthetic context. The presence of these values in literary works does not change them (a dignified ode style does not change the nature of dignity), and equally literature cannot be divorced from them. We are always faced, not by a theoretical aesthetic construct, but by a work together with its ambience and system of connecting links. The evidence supports also in the strongest manner the proposition we made early in the argument, that interpretative judgements within the framework of functional consanguinity are more adequate than others, because they derive from finer and more searching comprehension. It is a commonplace of language theory that a great deal of speech relies for understanding on a network of unspoken references, of meanings not directly expressed verbally. Something of a similar kind happens with literature, and more with some styles than others. For instance, much romantic poetry (Byron, Victor Hugo, even Wordsworth and Goethe) depends on the reader having an emotional sounding-board of the same type as the poet himself. In other words, there are certain implied affective factors the poet does not need to make verbally explicit. The unpopularity of the romantic rhetorical style today is due to the absence in readers of the same set of overtones on which the poet at the time of writing relied. In consequence one can say that such poetry is not properly apprehended, and negative judgement inevitable, but inadequate. All works and styles depend on latent emotional dispositions of this kind, and these relationships are in fact an aspect of function.

Finally, the idea of a function or functions for literary works raises two problems of a special kind about which a word must be said. One concerns popular literature, and the other, propaganda.

It could be objected to the argument of this chapter that popular literature plays an exactly similar functional role for its enthusiasts, and that this is damaging to the idea of literature having a special quality, as also to the problem of judgement, which becomes confused and obscured if we allow importance to personal taste even when vulgar. It seems on the surface to reduce everything to the level ground of 'what I like is good for me'. There are two answers to this objection. In the first place we recall our premiss that the problem we are dealing with starts *beyond* the demarcation line of good and bad literature (non-literature). I am seeking a more discriminating analysis of the nature of personal taste in relation to sophisticated evaluation. The second reply is that the similarity of function here in question is one of the real links between high and low art. The problem as to what jazz shares with classical music, novels with novelettes, fine painting with popular, recurs in studies of aesthetics; and whenever the search for absolutes dominates the problem, or the desire to isolate effectively art from non-art, it is a stumbling-block. But it is not essential to make this total differentiation; they are all art of a kind. Popular art does not degrade high art by fulfilling a similar function, any more than homely parables do great ones.

About the second problem, propaganda, we note first that for some people the notion of propaganda art is a contradiction in terms, because the aesthetic should be disinterested. For others, more practical and compromising, it is simply the application of literary skill to a purpose, as in war effort, politics, or advertising; it is a use of art, of an obvious kind. Where the message to be put across is simple, as it normally is in the best directed and most effective propaganda, two apparently opposite reactions can be produced; you are subdued by the conquering message and overlook the art; or you are impervious to the message, in which case the art applied may be thrown into relief separately from the purpose. The ideal case should be, no doubt, that you believe in the message and admire the art used to project it. The interest for us, in the context of our argument about the function of art, is that in such cases the aesthetic factor is present and has a meaning, without being an end in itself.

It is often said in a loose way that religious art is a kind of propaganda, or that poetry propagates beliefs or philosophies. T. S. Eliot, for instance, wrote of Milton as a propagandist, and even Dante and Lucretius before him. This way of speaking always leads on to the vexed question of intrinsic poetic values in relation to the so-called propaganda element; critics then begin to dissociate the two and look at the work 'as poetry', as they say. I do not like this use of the word propaganda, because the statement of a philosophy in poetry is not necessarily an act of propaganda. To write a poem which includes a statement of thought or philosophy is not the same thing as to write a poem that is intended to, or actually does, propagate that philosophy in the strict sense. In this connection the word is used imprecisely. No doubt the strong statement of any belief may imply the desire to convince, which is a slightly different emotional situation from the simple motive of stating for oneself what one holds to be true. There is, however, a gap between enthusiasm for one's own beliefs and values, and the attempt by rhetorical persuasion to change a reader's views. And there is a still further gap between this and the incitement to action rather than thought, which is the true motive of propaganda. The essential aesthetic problem is the difference between a statement of thought purely and simply, and a poetic statement in which thought is a constituent of the statement. But whether thought or propaganda is involved I think analysis should begin by saying that the work is a poem (novel, drama) and then assign it to a type of literature, in this case a didactic or parable form. This is better than looking at the philosophy first, and then going into the defensive position of the argument 'but if we look at the work simply as poetry . . .'. This way of proceeding really implies that you are now going to apply not merely a strictly poetic test, but a different conception of what poetry is. It might be, for instance, that you are approaching with the symbolist conception in mind; yet it would be quite misguided to judge a remote didactic or philosophical poem by the symbolist aesthetic.

The loose application of the idea of propaganda meets us also in connection with types of literature with a strong social philosophy, as in the earlier comedies of Shaw, for instance, or the political and social satires of Dryden, Swift, or Samuel Butler. Mentioning such works gives a hint of a border country where the simple expression of ideology in literary form shades over into propaganda. There are many cases where works imply beliefs without actively propagating them, and also many others where activation is stronger. This might be true of vigorous revolutionary writers like Schiller, Büchner, Brecht, and Sartre. In accordance with the argument of this chapter about uses of literature I would certainly accept that a work about revolution—Schiller's *The Robbers*, for instance, famous in its day and taken by Tolstoy into his canon of brotherhood literature—is from one point of view not only a piece of expressive writing. It goes further than that; it is expressive *behaviour* in the author; it is rhetoric, and the twin of action. People who never feel revolutionary do not muster enough interest to write a revolutionary work. But with powerful poetic or dramatic talents like Schiller, Büchner, or Brecht a play is not only subjective, exclamatory, and aimed at rhetorical persuasion, but it objectifies a context of revolution and revolutionary characters. The author may communicate inflammatory feelings, but he also works something into a clear image. His play is then a genuine representation, and not just a piece of propaganda.

A point I want to clarify, however, is a difference between art and propaganda that is crucial and makes it impossible to confuse the two. It is essential to distinguish between poetic works based on given beliefs (like the work of the metaphysical religious poets), susceptible in consequence of fulfilling a natural function for readers who share those beliefs; and works which aim to convert unbelievers to views not previously held. The function involved in the former case is organic, legitimate, genetically and causally natural, and necessary. In the latter case there is an imposed didactic purpose. In the former there is an invitation to truth; the truth of a body of belief, and the truth of self, as this self embraces the truth in a congruent spiritual act. The result of this is a genuine ceremony or ritual, uniting author, work, and reader in a total *credo*, and in a natural harmony. In propaganda, by contrast, truth is often distorted, contaminated, or neglected; there is a design on the moral will that is more important than evolving truth, harmony, sincerity, and natural union. Propaganda embodies the assault of one will on another, irrespective of good or evil ends, and its sign is a rhetoric of persuasion of a quite deliberate kind. Even if it begins in truth it shoots beyond it, or distorts it, in the aggressiveness of its interest.

4

THE MOTIVATION OF CRITICISM

IN foregoing chapters I have attempted to clarify the problem of criticism and taste by approaching it not from the logical positions raised by the desire for objective criteria but from the practical experience we commonly have, that literature functions for us in different ways. This led to the suggestion that two prominent strains of criticism (a criticism of affinity, and a criticism of debate) arise from the two main attitudes to literature discussed. About these more must now be said.

It will be useful to do this, however, within the framework of the general question of motivation in criticism, which is rarely examined directly. Motivation is in fact complicated. The usual assumption has been that all criticism is a variant of a standard form, or rather of a uniform intention, which is to assess, or to interpret with understanding, or both; and in consequence critics, wishing to do their job properly, have always been dominated by anxiety as to what criticism *ought* to be, once it goes beyond the casual and spontaneous and seeks to be wholly responsible, consistent, and ideally adequate. Discussion of this aim raises immediately a cluster of questions which are of distinct kinds but nevertheless so interlocked as to be inseparable. The seemingly simple questions: Does this poem affect me? does it please me? is it a good poem—as an imaginative creation, that is, not only as a source of agreeable sensations—these questions are tied up with the more fundamental one, what *is* a poem? what *is* literature? as well as with others, some of them intricate philosophical questions, about sensation, perception, mental images, illusion, reality, and language; a network at the best, a thicket at the worst, of difficult concepts. It is, moreover, a great peculiarity of literary criticism that it has to define its object as it assesses, to assess as it defines. What writers on art often say nowadays, that the artist doesn't know what his work is going to be until it is finished, would apply with still greater force to the results of criticism, because of the fact that a *qualified* evaluation of a poem ends up as a detraction from its *status* as poetry. You start off your criticism expecting poetry and you find you have less than you thought; the object of criticism dissolves at its touch. Criticism differs in this from other forms of knowledge; you can, for instance, describe the subject-matter of history without having first to define it in an evaluative process. It is in the documents and reports; crude, but there.

In spite of these great difficulties, however, the notion of an ideal, objective criticism, combining analysis, impartiality, and understanding, continues to be propagated, with the implication that anything less than this must be invalid. There is also another, equally exacting implication; it is that all truly worthy reading carries criticism always to its full deployment, and that a literary work, to be fully worthy, must be able to sustain the rigour of such a standard. Fortunately literature is much more generous, much more human, much more indulgent, more capricious, more secretive and mysterious, and more diplomatic, than the practitioners of this kind of idealism, which is too restrictive in its consequences.

To do justice to the larger situation it is essential to conceive of differing motives, varied purposes, and of correspondingly divergent kinds of criticism. This is not, let it be stressed, to distinguish methods of criticism; the point is a distinction of motive, and of purpose, in the manner of commenting, which produces not simply different methods but different types of criticism, each with its own justification. They all represent, in my view, a natural, spontaneous mode of comment, oral in the first place, then written and formal; but we shall note that some of them have been institutionalized.

The primary and most spontaneous kind of criticism is the act of deciding whether a work has quality or not. This follows on the immediate reactions when reading; it occurs at many levels of knowledge, critical skill, and sophistication. It is so natural an activity that to speak of motive in connection with it is to suggest a deliberation or self-consciousness not really present. But if one is to ascribe a motive to it, it would be, surely, the desire to express a rational confirmation that one has had a genuine aesthetic experience, or that one has had only a defective one. It is, of course, eminently practical, in that it helps you to decide whether it would be profitable to read more of the same work, or author, or kind of writing.

But for all its naturalness, its being practised by everyone who reads at all, it is not simple or easy. Faced by a new poem, or novel, even experienced readers can find themselves plunged into the intricacies of judgement, turning over several, or for that matter, all of the urgent problems: the questions of feeling and ideas, of form and theme, of mimesis and expression, of description and evaluation, of subjective and objective, and so on; because many good works, and all only partially good works, do raise all the problems.

Some of these problems are dealt with in Part II. Here we need only say briefly that it is reasonably possible to establish some objective criteria, though it is best attempted at the most general level, and understood as a preliminary to detailed evaluation. I mean this rather in the sense in which we declare someone to be educated without becoming involved in the particularities of different ideals of education; or in the sense in which we speak of goodness without specifying the ingredients that make it up in any individual case. Many, even most, works make a predominant effect which is fulfilled as we complete the reading, and to apprehend it we do not need to stare at the details. For many this main effect is a sufficient pleasure, and there is in reality no obligation on any one individual to search beyond it with many of the works he may read. This fact, however, does not have a place in the theories of professional analytical evaluation. It is important, nevertheless. It is the basis of a great deal of agreement in judgement, by contrast to the disagreements generated by controversy over the problems of detail. It is also a godsend to authors, whom it provides with a wide audience more cheerful than the over-conscientious, anxious analyst.

A second motivation appears with the professional adjudicator, whether he be a good journalist or a good academic scholar. The distinguishing marks are ready knowledge, wide experience of books, and rational confidence; and these are applied with urbane discretion. Criticism of this kind is based on the primary judgements and general criteria referred to above, combined with a catholic sensitivity and receptivity, which ensure a generous, tolerant response to a great range of literary qualities and personalities. In the operations of a practitioner of such criticism all the criteria ever evolved, and the sense of varied values and qualities, will be welcome tools, valid and acceptable wherever appropriate. Considerable numbers of people have a disposition to this kind of catholicity; it is founded in a hedonistic attitude and broad human sympathies. It is institutionalized, firstly, in the professional criticism of the better press-journals, which has the prominent function of offering guidelines to the educated reader; and, secondly, in conventional literature syllabuses in schools and universities, though the hedonism is there overlaid with educational idealism. The idea behind it is that there is such a thing as 'purely literary' experience which may be culled anywhere, regardless of thought or beliefs. Because of this institutionalization it is often looked on as *normal* criticism, which is erroneous, since it is only one kind.

The third and fourth motives to distinguish are those leading to the two prominent strains of criticism indicated in our argument above. One of these, the 'criticism of affinity', which produces the most *adequate* interpretations and appreciation, the greatest illumination in affirmative assessment, needs no further comment; it has a clear, single, well-directed purpose, to elucidate and admire. But the other, the criticism of debate, must be looked at more closely.

This is a type of expert criticism which is a sophisticated mixture of assent and dissent, approval and reservation, acceptance and rejection, in the reaction to a work. Out of this emerges a great volume of written and spoken criticism, both of new work and of old, which may also be held by many educated readers to be a norm. I have argued above that in the course of reading a variety of works from the general motive of literary curiosity we become aware of gradations of enjoyment and approval, and form naturally a selection which is then seen to represent our own taste, our own literature of affinity. The type of criticism under consideration is that arising from the wide variety of reading in the corpus of literature on the impulse of curiosity. It is a criticism that reveals not our personal *selection* but our personal *view*; our opinions about many and varied authors and their works. It is a criticism of debate and positioning.

This strain of criticism throws up constantly and alarmingly such wide differences of opinion that two questions repeatedly arise and lead to ever recurrent discussion; first, with such differences, is it possible to believe in any objective, impersonal criteria whatever; and secondly, what *ought* criticism, if it is to be valid generally, to be and do? The first leads to all the theoretical discussion about standards of taste and criticism, the second to discussion about the true function of criticism. These questions imply lurking dissatisfaction with criticism at large, and the desire to purify or correct it. It drives many to the view that only interpretative criticism, in the spirit of understanding, is desirable or valid. C. S. Lewis implied this when he pointed out how futile mere debunking is. Many hold that if a work is assessed positively by some critics, any negative judgement of the same work is unhelpful, unimportant and inadequate. They would accept as a logical consequence that the criticism of explication puts any *less* adequate evaluation out of court.

But the point to scrutinize here is the plural purposes of criticism, especially of the literary classics; in fact, the perfectly sympathetic appreciation, or the perfect assessment, or the appropriate historical evaluation, belong only to one side of criticism, though in academic circles two or three decades of New Criticism and emphasis on the aesthetic object have laid a great stress on them. In reality, whether we think it logical or appropriate or not, criticism extends far beyond interpretation, appreciation, and assessment in the narrow sense. Its business includes a natural process of self-explication as well as author-explication. The criticism of debate reflects a form of philosophical, or ethical, or cultural positioning. It is based on beliefs, emotional attitudes, varying aesthetic sensibility, and theory, and cultural contexts, which differ greatly between individuals, and which, above all, occur in an infinite number of patterns and combinations. The effect of this is not absolute disagreement but something much more complex. It is a question of the essential, necessary partiality of all judgements, and of the patterns of overlapping fragments of opinion. Judgements are partial in the sense that they are either judgements of parts or aspects of works, rarely of wholes; or in the sense that they are subjectively conditioned. And the patterns of overlap always involve, as between critic and critic, or reader and reader, some agreement on some values, and some disagreement on others. It is essential to re-establish, or at least to stress, the view that this type of criticism produces a body of argument and public discussion which is directed not only to aesthetic explication but to the defence of independently held positions and of value-patterns transcending single works and single authors. In other words criticism is not only a secondary activity applied to literature, but is a form of independent thought. It is easy to accept that such criticism is not adequate *in the same way* as explication, as the appreciative criticism of affinity. But is that the only relevant factor? The criticism of debate has a different function in the total context of thought about literature.

This type of criticism is the natural sounding-board for the public character of literary works. Since Eliot, and Valéry as well, with the authority peculiar to creative artists, conceded that a poem, once launched on the world, may develop meanings not necessarily envisaged by its author, there has been easy acceptance of the idea that a poem may have or acquire variant meanings. There are clearly innumerable possibilities of varied response and varied overlap of interest between one work and many readers; in consequence of which we may say that any given work consists, for the world and the public, of itself plus an unlimited number of reactions to it. All conceptions of a work, or reactions to it, are part of its *public* identity, just as an individual is a private self plus his public resonance. Thus we can say that criticism, in its total extension, is the verbal formulation of the public identity of a work. Only in criticism so understood can all the variety of overlap and response be adequately analysed, accounted for, and justified.

Given the reality of variant meanings and evaluations, a consequence is that professional critics have to deal with both works and their variant meta-existences, whilst amateurs and naïve readers can simply maintain a direct author–reader communication-line. It is very difficult to say that such a link, which, like all communication, may be only partially effective, is less satisfactory than professional knowledge of a work plus its interpretative variants. The latter give knowledge of other readers and not only of the work. Interpretations are always distortions—distortions from one person to another, one pattern of connections to another. In the distortion lies the interest. If we do agree entirely with a critic's interpretation of a work we have the pleasure of agreement and confirmation, which is sometimes valuable, certainly so when we are still relatively inexperienced and wish to learn. But the agreement adds nothing to what we knew for ourselves; and so is from one point of view unnecessary to us. This becomes plain to us in later experience. Criticism, on this count, is more interesting if it states differences of view. Such interest, however, should arise from natural differing and not from affectation. A critic, in differing, must be reasonable, and not fanciful or outrageous or gimmicky. In short, his own connections of meaning, into which he places someone else's poem or work, must in themselves make sense and be worthy of consideration. All the notable critics had such a good system of connections, or a set of values of their own, or a strong point of view, which they in fact propagated under a guise of interpreting and assessing other men's works. Johnson, Coleridge, Herder, Taine, Eliot, all proceeded in this way.

What we have to come to terms with here, moreover, is a double root of diverse opinion. On the one hand, a work is actually perceived and understood differently; and on the other, judged and criticized differently. Even if one argues that all readers should at least try to observe a work purely and steadily, eliminating consciously as many verbal misunderstandings and prejudices as possible, so that from one point of view an approximate agreement might be achieved, there remain the innumerably varied contexts of intellect, sensibility, experience, values, and world-view, upon which the work impinges with each separate individual. Here no approximating process is possible. For now the work is not so much the *object* of diverse opinion as the *occasion* of bringing it out into the open; it focuses pre-existent views and ideas of various kinds, and focuses precisely their incompatibility. The individual reaction involves, with intelligent, thinking persons, *all* the intellectual and spiritual contents of their mind, in consequence of which an infinite variety of problems may be sparked off. In short, all criticism that is evaluation in the broader sense, going beyond the simplest aesthetic judgements, is a veiled self-explanation, self-presentation, and self-justification; and therefore essentially and profoundly polemical. It is in this aspect that criticism is basically, as we said above, a form of philosophical positioning, or values-defence, and not a search for agreed judgement. (Under 'philosophical' I include any consistent system of values.) In this process both individual positions and also areas of group-agreement may emerge, the latter on the basis of the cognate, each individual finding his own group or groups, his own affinities and alliances which constitute his base for critical polemics. Criticism always includes, when it is actually practised without submission to an anxious theory of what it ought to be, comments on any of the contents or references of a work. It covers the aesthetics of form or expression, but overflows and extends beyond them, constantly passing over, as Eliot said, into what are called other subjects or fields, such as morals, or history, or religion, and so on.

Criticism seen thus is a more positive activity than some writers allow. Mr. Righter, for instance, in *Logic and Criticism*, favours a liberal, non-dogmatic open-mindedness about the making of judgements. He holds that it is undesirable for criticism to be influenced by too definite codes or criteria, and he puts his faith in a general notion of 'reason-giving'. He is persuasive in arguing how, given the enormous variety of criticism, it would be undesirable to have either rigid concepts for evaluation or very uniform reactions followed by monotonously similar and repetitive judgements. This view is acceptable up to a point; yet the open-mindedness could look more like an avoidance of committal to something than an argued defence of variety in criticism. The latter is not substantiated or justified as a positive phenomenon or process, but seen merely as something one has to let happen. My view is that we must go further than this and accept that criticism, in one dominant form, transcends explication and aesthetic assessment and becomes an independent activity. Critical statements not bearing exclusively on sympathetic appreciation have an added existence and value as part of the vast conflict of ideas and beliefs that all people who think and write and talk wage with each other all the time. Though sparked off by reaction to single works, they show critics, students, people, all of us, arguing our own point of view, our own interpretations and comments in connection with any of the ideas brought into play by the work. They show a philosopher in everyone, fighting for his own system of values or *Weltanschauung*. As such, as evidence for a possible position, as support for an individual view, all this criticism is both legitimate and interesting. Here we have the real reason why it is valid and useful. It is a clarification not simply, and not narrowly, of one work, or one author, or one literary principle, but of many problems, many hypotheses, many attitudes and ideas, relevant certainly to any particular work or author under scrutiny, but far beyond that, to the whole field of ideas. Mr. Righter, anxious to evade dogma, or sterile, restrictive criteria, suggests that the manifold work of criticism is good simply as a process, and not as something that necessarily leads to definite conclusions; indeed, he takes the view that it is not desirable for such conclusions to be reached, since they might turn out to be rigid and dull, too much of an abstract compromise, if all are to reach agreement. Against this view I would say that the mass of varied criticism helps each individual to reach conclusions of his own, which is what matters. For though it may not be desirable to render conclusions vapid for the mere sake of wide agreement, it is surely good to reach some sort of conclusions. Each one of us can do so. Each one of us does, unless we are happy to be passive, submitting to every wind that blows, and without character of our own. This indicates sufficiently, perhaps, what I mean by ascribing positive value to literary judgements essentially in conflict. They function within the largest framework of the philosophical debate on values.

A further comment is called for. Understood in the narrower, and simpler, sense, what we have just been saying refers particularly to the part played in criticism by a philosophy or world-view; an example is the case of T. S. Eliot's attitude to romantic poet-philosophers, or of Marxist critics to literature in general. But it is not so common now to hold anything so definable as a philosophy. Many rely on a sense of values, the positive presentation of which remains mostly in abeyance, without that necessarily suggesting woolliness or insincerity. This has a bearing on our present problem, however, because, as we said above, people of this inclination often seek their values either in literature, or through it; which means that an aesthetic factor, as distinct from the philosophical in the straight sense, enters into their assessments. 'Values', in this context, means often a mixture of non-aesthetic and aesthetic factors, and in any case the notion includes, as a value in itself, and as a feature of the humane outlook, the habit of mind and mental outlook characteristic of many poets and artists.

This phenomenon brings us into sight of a further motive and another type of criticism, which is highly original and independent. This sort of criticism—names like Winters, Tate, Eliot, come to mind—is usually an idiosyncratic synthesis of (1) primary judgements, (2) philosophical attitudes, and (3) a preference for certain qualities over others, for values moral, vital, and aesthetic in special combinations. Such a synthesis signalizes an individual *taste*. A combination of this kind makes a *set* of criteria, each member of which may be perfectly general and impersonal in itself (for instance, the criterion of 'spontaneity', or formal invention, or 'complexity', or 'maturity'), whilst forming a personally determined pattern when brought into conjunction with others. I am avoiding the terms objective and subjective as much as possible, because I think they are misleading: they establish an unnecessary, rigid dichotomy. The values critics discern and define are impersonal, and non-subjective; they exist independently of individuals. A value such as centrality of form is not a subjective phenomenon, nor is a very different kind of value, the sense of intense life. But a grouping of selected values, a set of criteria, as here described, is personal; it is a pattern of objective values, the grouping of which is subjectively conditioned; it is a personal taste-formation on the basis of impersonal values. This cuts across the question of 'right' or 'wrong', 'good' or 'bad'; it replaces these crude opposites. Eliot, for instance, combines a number of general notions, the sense of tradition, of classicism, the basic objective correlative, and the sense of poetic renewal through contemporary speech idiom, which gives contact with real life, and genuine, as against assumed or rhetorical, feeling. These and other recurrent factors make a criteria-pattern to which most of his evaluations of particular poets can be referred, and it produced the shaking-up of habitual rankings that was sensational in the twenties and thirties. John Casey has devoted a chapter in *The Language of Criticism*[1] to the implications of Yvor Winters's requirement that poetry should 'make a defensible,

[1] (London, 1966), chap. VI, pp. 120 ff.

rational statement about a given human experience . . .' and
its associated emotions; which implies criteria, to be used for
ranking; and Winters has done some very radical reassessments
of romantic and post-romantic poetry with their help. The
same writer also discusses very fully and clearly the emergence
in F. R. Leavis's criticism of terms that occur in significant
'groupings', such as intelligence, self-knowledge, maturity; and
he gives a table of 'words associated with "life" in *Revaluation*',
this set of terms being the grounds for more positive, or more
adverse, assessments.[1]

A critic who works out a value scheme in this way is not
making only aesthetic discriminations, nor is he engaged in
self-abandonment in devoted elucidations. He may, and with
the degree of originality involved usually does, make illuminating general comments on poetry; but he is essentially engaged in
affirming a set of values that in fact refer both to poetry and to
life, and the problem of how to live and experience living. A
set of criteria, a values-pattern, evolves with apparent ration-
ality, to judge from its statement as criticism, but in fact
derives from deep instincts, and provides the basis both for the
approving delineation of the positive example and also for
'distanced' criticism of other authors and works. Such criticism
is not simply evaluative aesthetic criticism; it is classification, or
ranking, on a reasoning from a personal taste. It produces a
constellation (a) of qualities, and (b) of authors, which together
form the syndrome of a philosophico-aesthetic creed, though it
is never stated as a creed in so many propositions, but put
forward as 'criticism' having general validity.[2]

Finally, another motivation for criticism is historical interpretation and assessment. This appears often associated with
intensive, sympathetic elucidation. Some may think of it
simply as a logical step for criticism to take in the business of

[1] Ibid., pp. 156 and 177–8.
[2] The following comments of Barbara Hardy on James and Lawrence illustrate
the point very well: 'In James we find aesthetic values at their purest and most
extreme; in Lawrence we find the violent rejection of any external artistic values of
form and a passionate defence of particular truths. James rejects the loose, the
accidental, and the arbitrary, Lawrence rejects the fixed, the deliberated, the
conventional. Both of them use literary criticism for similar purposes of explaining
and publicizing the individual values they prize as novelists, and in the process of
idiosyncratic interpretation and judgement often do less than justice to other
writers.' (B. Hardy, *The Appropriate Form* (London, 1964), p. 132.)

elucidation. But I think the historical sense, as something independent, can run parallel with a literary interest, and from this angle it appears as another motive of literary study, leading to a distinct type of critical writing. We might distinguish two aspects; on the one hand there is the natural story of writers and works, showing their fortunes with their own contemporaries and with posterity; and, on the other, the attempt to reconstruct the literary past as past, as period, as history, differentiated from the present. The character of successive periods, linguistic usage, changes in concepts and the use of key-words, the background of social history, contribute to the picture thus made, providing the material for a vast scholarship. This, too, has now become institutionalized, and may in fact lead to some distortions in our attitude to literature, its reality, value, and function.

Under this head we ought perhaps to say a word about the *Kulturkritiker*, the critic who interprets literature as a constituent of general cultural trends, as they are seen in historical contexts. Where an idealist notion of culture as the creation of values operates, the critical process consists in literary works being scrutinized and ranked, and the best taken to be the essential expression of the age. Looked at in a conspectus they represent what the culture of a period at the creative level is. Where culture is taken more in its anthropological meaning, however, the strictly poetic ranking is less pronounced; here somewhat wider ranges of works may be interpreted as characteristic aspects of the period. A very large number of critics work without any doubt whatever on the assumption that literature provides a set of documents for the life of any given time or period and its interpretation by sensitive minds. What such critics do, in fact, is to take all these documents in their interrelationship and by means of them interpret the character of a culture at a given moment. This constitutes for them the principal significance of literature, and it gives them as critics their own particular dignity and original function. They interpret the whole; they make the assessments of values and of the conflict of values; they thus do what no single author can do, since he is only working his own corner. A significant author for such critics is one whose statements can be seen to fit into a more comprehensive scheme.

Some critics motivated in this way often concentrate their attention on contemporary or 'modern'—an elastic term— literature. They then use literary criticism as a base for an added cultural commentary of their own. They interpret contemporary, and pre-contemporary, literature as the index of the cultural climate, and then, going beyond the limited brief of the pure literary critic, propound value-criticisms, or a value-system, of their own, doing their own bit of moralizing or preaching, judging the time and showing a better way.

It seems to me important to understand what I have called the motivation of these types of criticism. They are distinct activities, springing from different desires, and each has its own relationship with literature. They each present judgements, but the act of judgement takes a different form with each, and has a different origin and function. Judgement, evaluation, criticism, are not one thing but several. To say what criticism is, or ought to be, without taking account of this diversity, is not likely to succeed.

5

LITERATURE AND EDUCATION

THE views we have been expounding suggest that we must revise some traditional notions of the role of serious literature in education, and in the economy of civilized society.

We might conveniently start from the traditional nineteenth-century idea that literature was a branch of some Higher Teaching; that something of the function of prophecy and religion had devolved upon it; or that it was a criticism of life, a department of wisdom, a guide to nobility, all of which are secular deviations of originally religious things.

This view of literature was first promulgated in the early part of the century by romantic writers; Shelley's views on the function of poets as legislators are often enough quoted. The later nineteenth century carried this idealism still further under the pressure exerted on literature by declining religious faith; a substitute was needed, and Matthew Arnold's ideas on the role literature might play in filling the gap became representative. However, for my argument here, I would add the neo-classicism of the eighteenth century and earlier as another important influence on the development. The sense of classical literature as a corpus of exemplary writings, including philosophy and history as well as poetry, and making up a sort of second, secular, or pagan Bible, was reinforced by the nostalgic Hellenism of the romantics, and their sense of high prophetic vocation, to create finally an intensely luminous conception of literature and its place in human affairs. One could say that Arnold's famous phrase, which is a slogan-like phrase of the kind that pursue a life of their own far beyond their original meaning or context, a phrase, moreover, which tends to be understood as prescriptive, as pointing to a programme for literature, could be looked on as a summing-up of what the literature of the classics had stood for.

The notion of a corpus of classics contains an emotionally charged value-judgement of great potency. It was transferred,

as time went on, from ancient to modern literature, and gave
rise to the influential moralized view of literature as a classic
compendium of the world's wisdom. Literature was seen as the
storehouse of the finest thoughts of the human race, or even, in
more recent centuries, of a single nation. 'Everyman, I will go
with thee, and be thy guide, In thy most need to go by thy side'
was the motto of a famous edition of classics, printed on a scroll
amidst *Art Nouveau* decorative design inside the covers. What
often took place, of course, was, in relation to modern literature,
a selection from the large quantity of accumulated writing, a
selection made consciously and unconsciously in accordance
with, or under the influence of, current moral assumptions.

In this way literature gained a quite particular moral title.
Therewith its place both in education and as a spiritual
education, *in lieu of* religion, was made self-evident. It is the
basis of all moralist critics, and of humanist positions such as
that of Irving Babbitt in the early years of this century. I think
we should also remember in this connection the practical fact
that one could, in the past, easily master literature understood
in this restricted way. The classical body of poetry and wisdom
was manageable; moreover, it was the classics as a whole that
mattered; that was the authority and the magic. One could, as
an amateur, read it all in a year or two, and one then knew
about man, his destiny, his recipes for coping with it, his
aspirations, his griefs, his tragedy and triumph. One knew
about the self-knowledge and cultural achievement not of a
few men, but of Man, the human race as a whole. This enormously reinforced the sense of the power of literature.

Such a conception is no longer possible or desirable. Literature is much wider in scope than either a classical (ancient and
modern) or a moral selection could be, and to make one would
be both a distortion and an impoverishment. Either of these
limitations would mean the loss of many of the possibilities
literature holds. Its variety, and variety of use or function, its
offerings of innumerable shades of value and pleasure, would be
lost. The problem of quantity too, which is increasingly urgent,
would be solved in too prescriptive a manner, even though we
admit that no one person can know anything like the whole of
canonized literature, not even of the sum of masterpieces, and
therefore must select.

Certainly selection is forced upon us, and will be still more in a future which by all appearances will bring increased populations, increased writing and reading public, and extended educational facilities. But whilst no one can know the whole, whilst everyone must select, any selection will inevitably be fragmentary. The question to face in our new situation is whether we should encourage a chaotic, meaningless fragment for each individual, or one with some sort of meaning. Do we accept simple accumulation? An endless procession of readings, each displacing the preceding, the whole disappearing behind one like footsteps in watery sands? Something of this will continue as part of the habit of reading and of curiosity; we can still accept Bacon's distinctions of intensity. But we can also believe that literature, even as a small selection, can nevertheless by virtue of its function for the individual be given a particular meaning.

The second factor in the present position is that the combination of aesthetic *and* moral as a joint standard has to be rejected as inadequate to the nature of literature; it was a feature of a particular phase of culture in the later nineteenth century, with no absolute truth in it.

In this situation we not only have the right, but we are under the necessity, of adopting new modes of selection. Rejecting a specific moral criterion as inconsistent with adequate aesthetic principles we are faced by the mass, the growing mass, of good literature. We might try to limit on the basis of masterpieces, but however practically useful this might seem to be we remember that even this area has undetermined boundaries and variable content from person to person. So the case for a deliberate development of personal taste towards an 'affinity' literature is unanswerable, so long as it is carried out on the twin basis suggested in preceding sections: the consolidation of a characteristic, defensible, taste concurrently with constant exploration and experiment. It is foolish to restrict oneself, as a moral duty, to the old idea of a literature of the world's wisdom in classical embodiment; and it is equally foolish to look on all literature as something that 'ought' to fulfil the conditions of wisdom and classicism. In short, one has the right, in good principle, to make a personal appropriation of the literature that is consonant with one's nature. One makes a personal pattern in which subject-matter, thought, temper, kind, and style have correlated value and significance.[1]

A problem remains, however, because in our new situation there is a gap left by the abandonment of the moral function implicit in a selective classical literature. It is an educational and cultural gap. I mean it exists both for institutional education and for the self-culture of thinking adults. Neither pure aesthetic training in literature, nor a professional specialism, an academic subject English Literature, can suffice as a *substitute* for a moral education. Arnold still thought in terms of replacing religion; we have gone a long way since then, for many now see literature as neither religious nor moral nor philosophical, but as something with a special character of its own, as a substitute for a set of principles, and as the conditioning basis for a liberal outlook. If one wants a broad and simple formula, literature is for many now a combination of truth and catharsis; it is document and emotional discharge, toning up the humane sensibility, but without necessary or explicit moral commitment. Yet literature cannot be expected to be a

---

[1] The most radical, and courageous, statement of the case for taking into account, in the educational process itself, individual variation of taste is to be found in Joan Evans, *Taste and Temperament* (London, 1939). Two passages are especially worth quoting; the scheme of psychological types they use may be open to criticism, but their essential point is valid: (1) 'The working artist can be trusted to find the medium that suits him best, the genre that he most loves to paint and the genre that he can sell most easily. The one field in which it may be of practical value is that of education. The artist will either work out his own point of view, consciously or unconsciously, or be a failure; the spectator may be driven by educational, social or critical influences into seeing things falsely, and his failure (though just as gross) will be less evident. It is the duty of every man to discover what works of art he truly admires, and the duty of every educationist to set him on the right path of discovery.' (p. 109.) (2) 'If we accept the fact that the natural reaction of each individual mind to the work of art must be respected, as a part of the human personality, and that spontaneity is an essential quality of artistic judgement, the element of compulsion in matters of taste must disappear from the teaching of the history of art, and from that dangerous educational enterprise known as "training in art appreciation". It is something that modern pacifists have decided that the Charge of the Light Brigade and the Death of Nelson are not the ideal pictures for schools: but no more—for the quick extrovert—are photographs of the Parthenon; or—for the quick introvert—reproductions of Raphael's Madonnas; or—for the slow introvert—some gay modernistic print from Germany ... [children] ... may be taught to look at works of art from the historical or technical point of view, but they should not be taught to admire what their teacher considers admirable.' (p.110.) There is a brief and pregnant reference to this problem in T. S. Eliot, *The Use of Poetry and the Use of Criticism* (London, 1933), in the 'Note to Chapter I, On the Development of Taste in Poetry', pp. 32 ff.

philosophy in itself. Some American critics (R. P. Blackmur, for example) have pointed out how there has been a tendency in recent decades, perhaps since the beginning of this century, to put the whole burden of culture, of cultural creating and consciousness, on to literature. Certainly one would agree that literary people, and perhaps some critics especially, have tended to think of themselves as the bearers of modern culture. But this is an error; an error in any case to conceive of one single branch of thought as the sole pillar of a culture; but also an error to think of a sceptical or morally diffident literature thus.

Literature cannot perform this task alone, and the logical consequence of the new situation would be to say: read literature, but also read ethics; read poetry, but also theology, or philosophy; read aesthetic objects, but also law and sociology. These things must intertwine before one can have a true culture, social or personal. Literature, like art, cannot of itself provide principles of behaviour, that is, of *mores*. In this respect it is scarcely better off than science.

It might be objected at this point that the moral influence of literature is not in fact direct, this being too crude a notion for something of its very nature so delicate. A strong argument, to which we would accede, can be adduced for literature as an agent of spiritual sensitiveness with a mode of operation more like that of religion than practical ethics. For this view a certain kind of elevated thought or temper, a certain effluence of nobility, or a power of refinement, would always be associated with the secret workings of literature on the psyche and the character. Poetry that deals with visions, drama that conveys the feelings of tragedy or the healthy rationalism of comedy, the novel as a delineation of conflict or suffering—they all contribute to a sensitizing of the mind, conscience and feelings, and so must be, in the broad sense, ennobling or at least humanizing.

All this is true, and yet it neither covers all that literature is and does, nor does it provide an effective rule of behaviour. And one has to admit that many modern adepts at literature, especially professional critics, students, and thoughtful public, understand their interest as one of liberal open-mindedness; they seek in literature confirmation and food for a certain sense

of difficulty, for an attitude of experimental, sceptical, inquiry into human situations, a recognition in fact, or a wish to
hold, that anything so definite as a moral rule, conclusion, or
judgement is a crudity inadequate to the complexity of life. In
modern life, moreover, it must be admitted that many people,
perhaps the majority, live by specialisms and various social
group techniques, by local understandings and loyalties, and it
is easy, when cushioned in addition by Welfare against what
were formerly common and frequent adversities, to be carried
along comfortably by a set of shared habits and assumptions
without having to formulate precise moral notions. Yet in the
sudden, unexpected crisis, the extreme situation, the victimizing
twist of circumstances, in which everyone may still be caught,
there is need of a guiding light, a good principle, a sufficient
reason, a deep conviction, a well-founded law, or a consolation,
which protect or give security. And literature, which like
science is imagination, not will, cannot necessarily give this.
Literature cannot be a simple substitute for a philosophy, not
even for a sceptical one. It is neither an instrument of morals
nor a part of moral education in the narrow sense. As for
knowledge *about* literature, that too, however intensely developed, cannot replace a philosophy of life; literary critics and
scholars cannot become society's magistrates or legislators. For
this reason we repeat that the individual needs both an
education in literature and also one in ethics, or philosophy, or
some creed.

However much one may believe ideally in the sensitizing role
of literature for mind and sensibility, only a little knowledge of
professional *literati* is required to reveal the extensive dis-
sociation between a thus sensitized mind, pre-occupied and at
work on literary material, and the moral behaviour of its owner.
The sense of spiritual or moral experiences and states of
consciousness may seem remote from Pater's aesthetic faith in
exquisite moments that contain the life worth calling real, but
they are, in spite of their apparent greater commitment to
something human, extremely similar as states of private or
inward contemplation. Many people, in other words, are
sensitized for the duration of the literary experience, but not
outside it. The life of their sensibility is one thing, and their
external doings another.

This actual state of affairs reinforces my argument that literature cannot perform the functions of morals in any simple sense. But also, as we said just now, it is not necessary for every kind of literature to have latent moral force. For an education however—which is our theme at the moment—patterns associating literature with other educational or cultural factors are highly desirable. Here the idea of literature functioning in congruence with a personal taste is relevant and fruitful. For a long time now the model offered by education and implied in a hundred ways by critics and scholars is the reader able to distinguish the literary aspects of literature abstracted from subject-matter, working with the oft-repeated tag 'but purely *as literature*, the work is . . .', expert at skimming off books an aesthetic, poetic cream. A better model is the reader who, whilst able to see in many places the symptoms of significant work, can above all integrate some of the literature he reads into a comprehensive scheme of his own beliefs. To read all novels, like the misguided scholar who wrote a universal history of the novel, for their significance 'as literature' is to miss, finally, the roots of significance. But introspective novels read alongside psychology, or novels of manners alongside social history and philosophy, make a living pattern for the reality of individual character and culture. Such links are more real than the tenuous literary or aesthetic links within the enormous variety of literature. What has the visionary devotional poetry of Vaughan in common with Jane Austen's novels, or Milton with Ivy Compton Burnett, or Laclos with Claudel? The 'as literature' idea is grossly overstated and unthinkingly taken for granted. Of course each kind, or section, or direction of literature isolated in this way is only a part of the whole; a religious taste obviously doesn't take in more than a fraction of literature. But a body of literature *for* a religious taste is a reality, just as a body of moral literature (the drama, for instance) is a reality for a moral taste. Religious thought, metaphysics, and prophetic poetry go together, as ethics, psychology, and the drama of moral conflict do. A literature of moral conflict, in either novels or plays, is a body of truth and ritual for a moralist or humanist; it would be an agnostic equivalent of sacred literature for the devout believer. In both cases literature exists in a larger framework than the passive aesthetic;

a functional use, which is of its essence, completes it in accord with a personal need and taste.

The problem I have been analysing, and for which I suggest a solution by integrating literature and personal taste, will become more important in the future. Literature and knowledge accumulate and increase in diversity with every increase in population and extension of education; and also with the increasing diversification of secular philosophies. There is more good writing than ever; there may on purely statistical grounds be more genius in the future; there is more journalism, criticism, scholarship and diffusion of knowledge; there is immensely more conditioning and flattery of comfortable taste. There is (1) a practical compulsion to select; (2) the need for an intellectual defence against sheer chaotic profusion; (3) the desire to maintain one's own individuality, *credo*, and style against annulment by the mass; and (4) the necessity to avoid false or outworn ideals or thoughtlessly accepted conventions. The better course is to let each individual's occupation with literature develop a character of its own, with its own claim to validity; he will then be saved from both supine aestheticism and superficial epicureanism.

PART II

6

QUALITIES AND CRITERIA

I T is not the intention of the following chapters to provide a
breviary of all evaluation, but to make some comments on
primary criteria. The former would be very intricate; if it could
be carried out at all, it would be a compendium of all the
techniques of criticism, and would cover both primary judgements and the elaborate processes involved in detailed assessments, the intricacy of which corresponds to the infinite
variety of literary works—variety of subject, of thought, genre,
language, and style. The average critical study of an author, or
collection of critical essays, nowadays consists normally of
detailed evaluations. They may of course still assess in a very
general way some of the virtues, qualities, and distinctive
marks of a work or author; but studies now, numerous, varied,
and professional as they are, tend to focus analytically on
special aspects of a work—the themes, the imagery and style,
the 'narrator', and so on. This sort of detailed evaluation
registers the strong, weak, and debatable features under
different heads. In doing so, it draws on a vast number of
qualities, and value terms, in order to clarify, describe, and
justify, the complex aesthetic experience of reading a given work.
Moreover, when critics speak of values in literary works they
often refer in fact to something much wider than aesthetic
values. They do not confine value to a set of qualities specifically
aesthetic, and which would operate as a group of criteria for
literary quality in the narrower sense. Any given work has its
own pattern of values and any author his own pattern, too.
When, in speaking of people, we give an admiring account of an
individual, his activities and achievements, what one might
call standard values (honesty, sincerity, acuteness of mind) are
only part of the picture; the whole includes many shadings and
combinations of qualities unique to this individual. For this
reason evaluation is infinitely varied and always transcends a
set of general criteria. But some of these will be valid. Similarly

in the case of literary works some general aesthetic and poetic criteria will be relevant. It is thus essential at the outset to make some distinction between specific *qualities* and general *criteria*. Wit and paradox, for instance, or irony, are qualities of some poems; but they are not criteria of poetry in general. In many historical styles, and certainly in the majority of true lyrics (highly musicalized poems), they are lacking, and indeed for many tastes impediments to the required effect. It is as with men; humility is a human characteristic, but not a criterion of man in general. So we must keep this distinction clear. Unity of effect, by contrast, is a genuine criterion; muddled composition, diffuse effects, irrelevancies, inevitably detract from an artistic conception. It would be impossible, and not very useful, to attempt to put down, and classify, all the qualities, all the valuable features, to be found by critical effort; but it is certainly helpful to clarify some primary criteria of general application.

It is in any case useful to recognize this important distinction between some principles that apply generally, and help one to say with confidence that a given work is a serious literary composition, and other criteria, which are often simply specific qualities, and which group themselves in subjective ways with different critics. These are what I would call secondary criteria; not in the sense of being less important, but of being supplementary, specific to some works and not to others.

What follows should be looked on as a series of comments on primary criteria. They will be non-technical, because they do not attempt to apply specialized philosophical analysis to the phenomena involved; they are not, in other words, technical aesthetics. They are intended to provide preliminary clarification of general service, and to indicate the foundation for the various types of criticism discussed in Part I.

7

COMMON MISUNDERSTANDINGS

A NUMBER of problems, uncertainties, and misunderstandings recur constantly in connection with criticism and its aims, making for difficulties that cause endless and fruitless discussion. Some informal observations on these at the outset might help to put the essential problems into a proper perspective.

First let us look at the view that judgements are immediate, or intuitive, that they depend in the long run on whether you have the right 'feeling' about the work in hand. We may have to admit that in questions of aesthetic something intuitive comes into play, if only because predisposition is involved. Nevertheless intuitive judgements about poetry only arise through a synthesis of intuition *and* training; on a higher level of trained taste, not on the lower level of simple naïveté. For the everyday use of this word 'intuition' is in this connection very ambiguous. I am not now referring to its technical meaning, as Croce, for instance, uses it in his aesthetic. Croce held the view that art altogether is intuition; i.e., the expression of direct, and not discursively derived, knowledge. What I am referring to is the ordinary rather loose use of the word, as when we say: 'I know this is a good poem—it is true I can't say why—I know it intuitively—I feel it.' Whoever says this sort of thing is either very naïve, or is forgetting too easily how our knowledge and experience of literature grow and develop through a long period of time. For the progressive formation of taste is a fact we cannot deny. We do not come into the world with our taste already formed. When we are very young we are only interested perhaps in adventure stories and we have probably very little sense for lyric poetry. Even when we have already discovered good literature it is the subject that engages our attention rather than the poetic qualities; we are more likely to get excited about plays and novels on topical problems than about classical works, and even if we do read lyric poetry we make a beginning usually with rather sentimental verse. In later years we have forgotten this transitional period; we forget it very quickly, in fact; but it did exist. Gradually, through natural opportunities for comparison which arise as one reads different works, through growing curiosity and repeated attempts with different books, we form from experience in a continuous process a schooled taste; the solid and significant displaces the shallow and crude. This process may well be at first unsystematic and fragmentary; it becomes more firmly and purposefully organized as we become more mature. The point is that it does take place. We then arrive at a stage when, as we read a poem or a text, we can judge it much more quickly and with more security—and this rapid passing of critical judgement is what we may then very incautiously call intuition. It is not intuition, and judgements of taste do not depend on a special organ that one either has or has not. These apparent intuitive judgements are judgements which may be made with great immediacy but only because of the habit, practice, repetition, and long experience, which have preceded them. But even a trained taste cannot in every case decide immediately whether a work is good or not. Assessment is always a matter of nuance; it is a difficult, complex process.

It is in this connection interesting to see how imprecise ways of thinking harden into stock ideas. A source of much confusion, and basically irrelevant argument, is the uncritically accepted idea that one forms a subjective view of a work on a single impression; as though a view were established by an instantaneous mental act. Subjectivity ('my' or 'your' view) is in fact very considerably modified by the necessity of each reader having to build up his experience of a work. The reception of a work is always an organizing of many impressions, recollections, associations, repeated viewings of detail; which occurs not merely by second and subsequent readings of the whole, but in the act of reading from the start, as the work accumulates for the remembering mind. This emphasizes its character as a complex act of thought; it is not a sensuous or perceptual experience in physical time, but is constructed in memory, in mental timelessness. Each time we look at a real landscape, a country scene, it really is a different scene we see; seconds or minutes have passed, the light has changed, we look at separate features in a different order, and the more we look the more it changes. A painting doesn't change; we simply see more of it, or something additional; and in this process we eliminate the momentary, or sharply subjective, impression. We lose our subjectivity and yield to the objectivity of the picture as it establishes itself for us outside the perceptual flux, as a construct of imaginative thought. Criticism, positive and negative, is inherent in this process. Evaluation builds up parallel to the building up of the work itself in one's mind. It is not one act, but a whole series, a continuous accretion of critical acts. Sometimes very skilled critics seem to give a total, finalized judgement; but it is very doubtful whether this can be so. The process is essentially unfinished, undeterminable, and a truly complete evaluation impossible.

Secondly, it is worth recalling very briefly how the notion of criticizing has, over the last two centuries or more, undergone certain conflicts, and has been, in the event, very much enlarged. In the earlier or middle eighteenth century criticism still meant judgement, its etymological meaning predominant; a critic of art or poetry was a judge. The conventions of form and genre were also of strong application; so that for the neoclassicist, familiar with the rules and the admirable classical models, criticism, positive or negative assessment, was a normative procedure. The lengths to which this attitude could be conventionalized are farcically illustrated by the story about Racine's comment after the first performance of his comedy *Les Plaideurs*: 'The audience was afraid it had not laughed according to the rules.' The first decisive change came with the literature of romanticism, when critics in tune with new ideas placed a sympathetic understanding of the poet's work and aims higher than a mere sitting in judgement on the basis of traditional rules. The new attitude hinged on the then novel conception of creativity in art and poetry, which meant that these produce something essentially original and by that very token not judgeable by previous work or old canons. This change in the emphasis of critical purpose was supported further by the increased respect paid to the idea of individual genius and personality, by the stress on the emotional, the irrational, and the mystical, and by general ideas of emancipation. But by mid-century another set of influences of equal power developed in association with historical studies and the sciences. As a result two main kinds of criticism dominated by about 1900, the impressionistic assessment, and a more severe, systematic method based on historical and scientific principles.

The situation for evaluation became confused, and led to much argument. We can perceive this in Irving Babbitt's essay on 'Standards in Criticism'.[1] The title itself is noteworthy, implying as it does a criticism *with*, and one *without*, 'standards'. His main concern is to reject the complete surrender to relativism and impressionistic opinion, but without going back to neo-classicism and its stiff adherence to something called 'the rules'. And indeed, it was a very real and acute problem. Remy de Gourmont might well say: 'La critique, c'est ériger en lois générales ses impressions personelles', but not everyone knows how to do that, and the total result of a great deal of impressionist criticism is usually a great deal of chaos and very little of general laws. Babbitt criticizes the impressionistic critic because he is too personal and his judgements too relative; he gives too much free rein to his temperament, and he is also usually too much of an epicurean. But Babbitt also criticizes the scientific critic, as he had emerged in the later nineteenth century. This kind of critic interests himself too little in actual evaluation; what he wants is to place the literary work into some sort of scheme, some relationship with other phenomena, which are usually historical, or philosophical, or social; and for him a work has significance in the degree to which it reflects the larger framework or context. Literature was not, in the work of such critics, evaluated as an aesthetic phenomenon for itself alone, but as one phenomenon amongst others in a broad historical development. Such was the positivistic study of literature, represented in extreme form by Taine; in it aesthetic assessment takes second place.

Babbitt's aim in his search for standards of criticism was to avoid the impressionistic, but nevertheless to evaluate the poetic as such. He doesn't want to be dogmatic; he wants a certain measure of freedom in matters of taste; but at the same time he wants to combine that with a discipline which does not derive from the individual, but is something impersonal, or represents an impersonal principle. Now the origin of this

---

[1] The essay, from *Masters of Modern French Criticism*, is reprinted in *Essays in Modern Literary Criticism*, ed. Ray B. West Jr. (New York, 1952), pp. 103–11.

principle he thinks he finds in something called 'the unity of human nature'. 'Good taste' meant, formerly, a compound of two things: individual sensibility together with the external rules which held the sensibility in check. The external rules having disappeared, Babbitt speaks of 'standards inwardly apprehended', of a 'literary conscience'. He cites Dr. Johnson: 'Do not, sir, accustom yourself to trust to *impressions*. By trusting to impressions a man may gradually come to yield to them, and at length to be subject to them, so as not to be a free agent, or what is the same thing in effect to *suppose* that he is not a free agent. A man who is in that state should not be suffered to live; . . . there can be no confidence in him, no more than in a tiger.' One must admit, this is extreme. Babbitt also refers to Brunetière's remark, quoted earlier, to a critic whom he thought too epicurean in taste: '*You* always praise what pleases you; *I* never do.' Babbitt himself wants a midway position; the right standard of criticism should certainly be in the individual sensibility, but should also transcend the personal self in 'the unity of human nature' (or what one man possesses in common with another). It is not clear how much this really says; and it leads Babbitt into a position where it is really 'posterity' that decides—the criterion is, does the work last? 'We should add, then, in order to define our critical standard completely, that the judgement of the keen-sighted few in the present needs to be ratified by the verdict of posterity.' Now the appeal to posterity, or to permanence, is not a prerogative of Babbitt; it is extremely common; indeed, it may be said to constitute the last-ditch stand when all other impersonal criteria have failed to convince. It is, however, basically a statistical principle; it appeals to the majority, in an intensive, even somewhat macabre sense; though most people who use it do not think of it that way. In my view it represents an abdication. One shouldn't have to gamble on posterity value; it is rather depressing to think that according to this principle one cannot oneself *know*, for certain, nor ever will, what is really good.

However disappointed we may be with Babbitt's solution we have to admit that he had observed a problem which became more and more important. Whatever criticism, or evaluation, may be, they became now part of, or at least associated with, a much larger apparatus of scholarship and interpretation. And it cannot be denied that there was in the sequence a tendency for scholarship to reduce the role of evaluation; to do without it even; simply to accept judgements from the past; and even in the name of history and 'knowledge' to make evaluation almost irrelevant. Wolfgang Kayser noted the point:

Literary historians write about, and evaluate, the literature of the past. They are generally silent on the subject of contemporary work. Don't they want to discuss this, or is it beyond their power? In the latter case doubts must clearly arise about their attitude to earlier work. It is at all events a simple fact that at the focal points of present-day criticism not much relation is noticeable amongst the scholars. Yet this reserve is not a tradition with them. We might remind ourselves that in the days of positivism, as it was called, the Deutsche Literaturzeitung carried a section in which E. Schmidt, H. Maync, and other leading academic critics reviewed new books. As a curiosity let us note that in 1903 E. Schmidt called attention with a special recommendation to the stories of the talented young writer Th. Mann. This column of the D.L.Z. disappeared in 1907, just about the time of the beginning of the *geistesgeschichtliche* (history of ideas) phase of scholarship. On this K. Viëtor wrote in 1945 a sort of obituary in the Publications of the Modern Language Association under the title: 'German History of Literature as History of Ideas'. A retrospect. Viëtor declared: 'For literary scholarship this extreme of the historical method had the serious consequence that the feeling for literary quality declined and with it the power of critical judgement.' This brings us back to our theme, as we wish to understand it: not as the general question of what kinds of evaluation are relevant and possible in regard to literature, but the specific question of the evaluation of literary art *as* literary art.[1]

W. Wimsatt also draws attention to the fact that the emphasis in the last thirty years has shifted from judgements (in the impressionistic sense) to analysis. The intention was good; one was trying to fasten on to something more consistent, more useful, more secure, that is, more scholarly and exact; but in practice analysis of this kind all too often relieves itself of the duty of evaluating. T. S. Eliot too, in one place, seems to support this process. He says that you give, as a critic, an analysis of a poem, trying to throw light on it thereby, and 'the reader is left to

---

[1] 'Literarische Wertung und Interpretation', in *Die Vortragsreise* (Bern, 1958), pp. 39–40 (my translation).

make the judgement'; that is, judgement 'looks after itself'. This may be so in the cases Eliot may have had in mind, especially cases of historical texts where some kind of preliminary knowledge is desirable for understanding. It is the case where the appropriate knowledge converts bland misunderstanding into understanding, upon which a true judgement becomes possible. But there are other situations for the business of evaluation, and we remember that Eliot himself as a critic has made some sharp judgements, on Milton, for example, on Shelley and Keats, and on Goethe.

We should not forget at this point what has been mentioned already, that there is a difference between primary judgements and detailed evaluation. The great range of poetic and literary expression calls for both kinds as the two stages of criticism; and since it is axiomatic that works are individuals, individual evaluative description alone can do them justice, if criticism has to fulfil itself to the utmost. The comparison with judging men and personality is valid; a description of character is interwoven with numerous value-judgements as qualities are reckoned up, and the pattern of qualities is always a mixture of general and particular qualities. A literary work, as an individual, is even more intricate. The qualities of the subject, of the techniques; all the intellectual virtues, the philosophical sensitiveness, the ethical assumptions of the mind at work, its modes of wit, curiosity, sensuousness, vision, and its command of moral emotions which we call compassion, nobility, dignity, serenity, renunciation, to name a few; all these aspects, echoes, repercussions, inherent characteristics, radiated forces, make up the field of values, and each work can be analysed, described, and evaluated in respect of them all, with a different pattern forming each time.

A history of criticism would show all the modifications and accretions of meaning the idea of criticism has undergone; I have merely given two or three examples. Clearly, the term used in relation to literary study has a much ampler meaning than in its everyday sense of a criticism of something said or done. It is not even reserved for complex evaluation, but made into an inclusive term to cover wide extensions of literary study. If we ask what is criticism, or what does it do, the answer is that it does many things, by the accumulations of practice over a long period of time. On the whole there is a vague assumption as to what criticism ought, ideally, to be; that can be summed up by saying that it should combine sympathetic interpretation, explication, elucidation, with evaluation; so that it might give both an enlarged understanding of authors and their work, and an assessment of merit, whether absolute or relative.

I think that in German the meaning of *Interpretation* in present-day usage is also an example of an amplification of a primary sense. *Kritik* tends to mean journalistic criticism, and *Literaturwissenschaft* a corpus of academic scholarship. *Interpretation* meant originally exegesis, the elucidation of meaning, and often involved the problem of alternative meanings. Now it goes beyond this, signifying an interpretative evaluation, or evaluative interpretation. Wolfgang Kayser has described the principles of this now widely used method:

The other method, to which we now turn, does not in the first place aim to evaluate. It takes a work as a single whole—this belongs to its conception of literature—and attempts to understand the structure of this whole and make it apparent. The method calls itself simply *Interpretation*. Interpretation is carried on wherever there are texts, indeed wherever there are meaningful forms. Interpretation is the analytical comprehension and exposition of semantic or functional unity in a structural complex. Interpretation views the elements of form in their functional relations. When we do not understand a word in a medieval text we look it up in a dictionary: that is not interpretation. When, on the other hand, Staiger and Heidegger find themselves arguing as to whether the *scheint* in Mörike's line: 'Was aber schön ist, selig scheint es in ihm selbst' ('But a thing of beauty is radiant and serene in itself') means *videtur* or *lucet*, they are engaged in Interpretation: from the context and back into the context, which in this case is first of all the meaning of the sentence, of the period, and then of the whole poem. Interpretation comes into play with anything relevant. Thus the aim of the method is to understand the mutual relationship and functioning of all the elements that go to the making of a unified total form: from external shape, sound, rhythm, words and diction, linguistic figures, syntax, events, motifs, symbols and figures to the ideas and significance, composition, perspective, narrative method, atmosphere (a concept . . . that has been especially well defined by the Englishman Wilson Knight), and all the other possible instruments of the form process. That particular forms like nouns, parataxis, oxymoron, etc., are not necessarily of themselves clear, so that they might be used as sign-posts to the core of the matter, is a basic assumption of the method. Altogether, 'interpretation' does not proceed from simple detail to larger complexity but moves constantly back and forth from part to whole and whole to part.

Now as structural harmony is progressively demonstrated it happens that we may also observe disharmonies and cracks, or that an element or complex fails to fit in with others and with the whole. In such cases the mere observation involves an evaluation, just as does the opposite demonstration of harmonious unity. No one, of course, will exaggerate details: minor blemishes never seriously disturb. Moreover, another question to put is whether disharmonies do not have a special meaning in the functional economy of the whole. Only when rifts and discrepancies in a work are deep-seated do they become relevant for evaluation.[1]

Interpretation undertaken in this spirit combines in a continuous process exegesis, appreciation, and aesthetic verification of structure.

Thus, at the present day, we have to deal with criticism in an elementary sense, with interpretation, and with literary scholarship. The first gives an appreciation, or a rejection, of a literary work or a passage, whereby the critic relies on general principles or recognized standards, or attempts to establish new ones, in order to rationalize the reactions of his sensibility. Interpretation attempts not only to interpret the word-sense, but to grasp, explain, and evaluate the whole aesthetic–poetic structure of a work at one and the same time. In the third place we see how literary criticism has gradually allied itself with other fields of interest, progressively; with historical problems, biography, philosophy and history of ideas, psychology, sociology, with studies on language and its function and conditions, and so on. And thus literary scholarship emerges from all these interests together. The varying combinations have in fact period character. Nowadays it appears to many students as though we had at last concentrated on the essential thing, namely the linguistic–poetic form as an autonomous phenomenon. But if one looks a little more closely one observes that this also corresponds to a general interest of our time. Literary expression is one kind of language, one kind of symbolism, one kind of meaning, one

[1] Op. cit., pp. 45–46.

kind of communication, one kind of consciousness; and these phenomena and processes are altogether in our time the object of special attention on the part of very varied thinkers. Philosophers, psychologists, anthropologists, theologians, and linguisticians themselves, have all shifted the emphasis of research from history and evolution to structural and psychological questions. Criticism is therefore in no way dependent only on literature; it, too, is influenced by general ideas and research aims of the age.

I would like to insert a passing comment at this point on a distinction which I think is real, but is not often discussed; it is in fact frequently overlooked. It is that criticism is one thing, and the writing of it another. We are all critics, in so far as we are readers; but some are writers as well. Everyone thinks a little, responds, has views, and talks; but some pursue their thoughts to a conclusion, think because they like thinking, are born to it, and like to see thought taken to its form in words. I think it is true to say that where this urge exists it has an energy of its own; a momentum that carries it beyond its subject in the strict sense; that makes it include in its motions other elements not springing exclusively from the actual deed of 'criticizing' a given literary object. Hence criticism, as it exists in the enormously extensive critical literature, includes far more than it might if kept to its chastest form, the ideal form people probably have in mind when they try to define what it is.

From all this we see that judgement in the simple sense is only a part of criticism, scholarship, and interpretation; yet it stands at the beginning of everything. As Helen Gardner says: 'The primary critical act is a judgement, the decision that a piece of writing has significance and value.'[1] However much knowledge you add up around literary works, you still have the problem of evaluation on your hands. Each time you read you are face to face with the questions: is it good, is it successful? *How* good is it? In what *ways* is it good? Or, looked at negatively, you say: something is wrong, what is it?

Let us turn now to two hardy perennials that come up in discussions about criticism; the pleasure factor, and the notion of perfection, or correctness, in works of art. The sense of enjoyment is certainly germane to art. People would not put themselves to the tedium and expense of long journeys to visit

---

[1] *The Business of Criticism* (Oxford, 1959), p. 6.

famous cities, museums, cathedrals, and palaces if there were not some keen pleasure in it. So too with poetry and books, which, when they do not please, do not get read. Indeed, enjoyment, and the impulse to praise what one has enjoyed, are the surest beginnings of articulate criticism; and negative criticism is, after all, the expression of disappointment at not finding the pleasure hoped for. One finds words for the features that aroused interest and enthusiasm, and one does this in the first place for oneself.

It is appropriate to remind ourselves that pleasure belongs to the process of evaluation. It is a mistake to think that we read good literature simply and solely because it is significant. There are people who by their nature take no interest in literature whatever, and derive no pleasure from it. Unable to do otherwise, they leave literature alone, and no amount of talk about its significance will do any good. There are, we must admit, areas of knowledge, philosophical, scientific, and technical, which are significant in a different sense, a social sense; they are important for everyone, because they are connected with our human and social needs, for which reason we are obliged to read and study them; for example, the medical sciences, many aspects of technology, the provision of food, water, sanitation, etc. Law, politics, and government may be added. All these subjects and sciences being necessities, the question of pleasure or otherwise does not arise. Religion, theology, history of religion, differ also from literature in this respect. They have significance for the life of man, and even sceptics read works in these fields because of their special significance. But with literature it is different; it must give a certain kind of pleasure as well as be significant. T. S. Eliot once said that it is better to engage in a closer study of a poem because it has pleased one, than to say a poem is good because one has given oneself a great deal of trouble studying it. Horace, Boileau, Pope, and many other critics have all remembered this particular aspect of poetry, that it should please, whatever else it does. We remember Kant's view, that the beautiful is that which arouses through its mere form a disinterested pleasure.

Now we can readily admit that it is much easier to say that literary works must please than to define the precise character of the pleasure so derived. Obviously, more than one type of pleasure is involved. One thinks to begin with of the famous aesthetic emotion which many critics refer to with enthusiasm as an infallible symptom. One thinks of the joyful pleasure that fills one as one looks at beautiful objects and reads beautiful poems. One thinks of the ecstasy about which Longinus wrote; he said poetry could be recognized from the fact that it does not simply persuade but transports. Many connect pleasure with a certain feeling of power and triumph which arises with the intellectual control, through form, of the world and human life. Life, with all its passions and feelings, happiness and grief, is transformed into image and form; it is sublimated; but a particular magic of literature lies in the fact that the energy and tumult of life still pulse through the tranquillity of form. We may mention further the natural pleasure we take in play, a relevant factor for which Schiller showed a profound understanding. There is also the natural pleasure we take in imitating, to which Aristotle drew attention. There is a point, moreover, at which the notion of pleasure mingles with a general sense of excitement, heightened effect, of quickened life or feeling, or of exaltation. And this in its turn does link pleasure with the response to enhanced or intensified subjects or effects, so that it becomes a very complex notion. The experience of literature is normally accompanied by one or other of a group of reactions such as the sense of intense illumination, the sense of wonder, the tragic emotion, feelings of human or moral aspiration, the sense of triumph in humour, comedy, and wit, the appeal of the exotic or of the supernatural, the fascination and horror of aberration and sin, the straightforward response to sensuous and formal beauty; all of which, together with many other reactions, form part of a general enveloping feeling of enhancement and elation.

These conceptions of pleasure are very general and not of a kind to be immediately useful to precise evaluations. But there must be pleasure; there must be some degree of 'ecstasy' if the reading of a literary work is to be an aesthetic experience. This ecstasy is not, as we said before, the only sign of a successful work, for one can become ecstatic by other means; but it is one sign amongst others and is therefore a factor in the critical process.

Turning to the notion of perfection, a good deal of misunderstanding in critical matters arises from the frequent and easy habit we form of coming to expect perfection from a literary work, indeed, to presuppose that this perfection must always be present; devotees of the method of interpretation or explication are not always aware of the extent to which they presuppose a perfect work. In reality perfect works are comparatively rare; and poets themselves know this best. We can really take it as axiomatic that evaluation is most often a matter of nuance and delicate assessment; it is rarely a question of black or white, perfect or imperfect. Perfection is most often to be seen in the shorter forms, in lyric poems above all. Edgar Allan Poe held the view that a literary work simply must be short if it is to escape the danger of being prosaic. In most longer works we find passages that are successful along with passages that are less successful; Horace drew attention to the fact that sometimes Homer nods. We are contented if longer works succeed as a whole, their total effect outweighing possible unsatisfactory effects of detail. For every work perfect in all its parts there are innumerable passages, single chapters, single stanzas, single dramatic scenes, that are good. Yeats declared that genuine poetry was extremely rare, but so infinitely precious that it was always worth reading a thousand lines in order to discover a few good ones.

Unevenness is a characteristic present to some extent in all literary compositions, some writers being particularly prone to it. This creates a problem for the inexperienced reader, especially one who is anxious to improve his taste. For we are naturally willing to give an obviously talented writer a good deal of rope, without falling into an uncritical surrender. So one has to learn the nuances of assessment even with good writers. But a more urgent complication arises from the stark fact, often forgotten where the study of literature leads to far more older literature being read than new productions, that poetic talent does not always exist in the purest forms. It is very common to have a little talent for writing, to have one or two of the group of gifts found in good writers; very common, too, to have a strong desire to write, without having all the gifts necessary. In this connection, with great works of genius in mind, we argue perhaps too often as though the various factors in literary creation were always evenly balanced. But in fact linguistic talent, or the ability to write stylishly, or technical command of certain forms, do not always go hand in hand with vision, or a message to impart. We do believe, in theory and ideally, in the inseparability of content and form, and critics are always talking about these or related terms, as they explain literary works. But let us not forget that this is really an aesthetic conclusion, inductively reasoned from *successful* works, which we may have in mind when we think of these problems. It seems to me that for the problem of evaluation the *process* of composition is as important as the result. Schubert said he had made his works out of his griefs and his technical musical knowledge. Valéry has described precisely how the poet has command over a technical apparatus—language, ideas, rhymes, images, metaphors, symbols etc.—with which he can conduct technical exercises. But then, in the moment when some meaning is seeking an expression, the appropriate words and images and symbols arise for him out of this apparatus, as though they had been waiting just for this moment. What we call genius is the ability to bring about this meeting of apparatus and vision as though it were the simplest and most natural thing in the world. A man who only has the one side at his disposal— only language, or only vision—is either a technical virtuoso, or a genius manqué.

The uneven distribution of the creative and technical talents, their capricious and often unharmonious relationships, produce great varieties of literary work which are difficult to estimate.[1] They in particular make evaluation into a peculiarly complex process, and this is especially the case with contemporary productions, which we have to judge entirely on our own with such skill as we have. Moreover, the most difficult cases are those where the miraculous conjunction referred to by Valéry almost occurs, but not quite, as, for example, in the work of writers like Galsworthy and Somerset Maugham.

In some ways the problem of judgement arises from a false aspiration. Many would like to be able to recognize good works of literature with absolute certainty. The question is to what extent this is really possible; perhaps we must put up with a degree of uncertainty. Certainly evaluation does not consist in

---

[1] I. A. Richards's selection of poems for the exercise reported in his *Practical Criticism* demonstrates the point vividly.

making one single intuitive decision. It is a progression, a sequence of reactions, judgements, and revisions; and this applies both for the individual and the general collectivity of readers. Evaluation must be considered as a complex and dynamic process. The important thing is not that works should be immediately recognized by everybody as masterpieces, but that they should be worthy of discussion. It is better to take part in this living process, even if one has to take risks, than to make anxious attempts to discover or invent a single theoretical criterion of miraculous efficacy. There is no point in just accepting values from the past and living amidst works that have been declared classics by others. One doesn't want to live either in a temple, or in a museum; the normal, intelligent reader is interested in exercising his judgement on a variety of literary works both past and present. In order to understand the problems of judgement effectively, moreover, one must be able to observe judgement operating throughout the whole field of literature and literary pretension.

8

MIMESIS AND VERISIMILITUDE

THE concept of *mimesis*, variously rendered as 'imitation' or 'representation', has a very long history since its starting-point in Aristotle. His preliminary insights, that imitation is instinctive in man, and that we receive a natural pleasure from imitations, are important and do not present much difficulty. Nor is it easy to deny that imitation, as in graphic art, in descriptive writing, in drama, miming, and acting, is a basic structural feature of art. Without mimesis most art would not exist. The generalization that in poetry the objects of imitation are the actions of men is also simple to accept in its generality. But Aristotle himself opens up some of the latent complications of this concept when he shows how there is not a single kind of imitation, but several, according to the means, the objects, and the manner. The numerous possibilities of meaning of this term began then to unfold in the Renaissance period and after, when art and poetry themselves, following on the medieval period, took on more and more diversified forms, and when sufficient evidence was already available that art and poetry moved between the poles of symbolic imagery or icons, which often involved non-naturalistic forms, and pictorial verisimilitude. We should, however, recognize that mimesis itself has natural latent symbolizing power. A secret of art, and also of one of the peculiar pleasures it gives, lies in a special combination: the use of devices, and the statement of visionary or intuitive truths. Mimetic representation is the most general and famous of such devices, and, taken in all its variations, the most frequent natural gift. It consists of the representation, by an actor, a painter, or a poet, of forms and appearances which resemble natural ones, but manipulated so as to address the mind with an added comment, thus creating a 'vision' by means of a device. Metre and metaphor are also such devices. One of the pleasure components in art and poetry derives from observing how these devices become fertile and active.

The problem we are concerned with here is not the technical aesthetics of mimesis but the part this idea plays as a criterion of judgement, more particularly in connection with verisimilitude and naturalistic forms. In an age like the last half-century when in painting and sculpture there has been a massive move away from figurative or naturalistic art, and in literature also a proliferation of expressionist, symbolical, and abstract-fantasy forms, it has become naïve to think of art or literature as simple representations 'of' objects, men, nature, or things; and no one now except the very untutored would use likeness as a standard of judgement. We have learned also, through the succeeding variety of styles, and associated aesthetic theorizing, to see the mimetic factor even in past art in an intertwined relationship with the expressive and the symbolic; we would never say nowadays that art is *only*, or even mainly, a mimesis; it always has a complex structure. Nevertheless, the imitation factor has not been eliminated. Certainly in novels and plays, however unrealistic, or 'anti-', there exist persons, actions, and events, which are referable to reality. And past art of a representational kind cannot properly be reconceived entirely on the lines of some modern aesthetic, whether symbolistic or expressionist. Moreover, in certain areas, a verisimilitude criterion will always have some degree of relevance. Portraits and landscapes are the straightforward examples of this, as the novel of manners, or the naturalistic drama of the nineties, are in literature. Apart from the simplest topographical drawings, there remains in all landscape a topographical element. The essential feature in portraiture is the visual definition of a given character, psychology, and personality. In course of time, obviously, portraits by great artists, when the originals are no longer known, are viewed simply as pictures. But their essential representational character is still operative; the degree of their particular verisimilitude is unknown, but their general human likeness is valid. Art forms of this kind have naturalistic representation as a main part of their aim, and they are then judged according to the fulfilment of the aim. If they are true to natural forms, either of particular persons or places, or in a general way, they are successful.

Mimetic verisimilitude is thus always in the field as a possible criterion; it cannot be ruled out absolutely. In the Renaissance

many intellectual interests helped to give art and literature
extremely solid naturalistic ingredients, which were a central
value, deliberately pursued. In painting, the discovery of
perspective started as a partly scientific interest, and it led to a
more vivid illusion of reality. Once introduced, the control of
perspective was expected of all good painting, and only ceased
to be so when, early in this century, it was deliberately rejected
for flat painting. The dramatic, literary subjects, from Bible,
legend, and myth, portraying a wide range of passions and
emotions with startling power, incorporated naturalistic truth,
like the portraits with their psychological analysis. Shakespeare's 'hold the mirror up to nature', and the realistic framework of the drama of the time, are corresponding literary
phenomena. Hamlet and Lear, Faustus and Edward II, are not
distorted dream images, they are not fantasies or caprices of
vision, but they are possible men, and the obedience to general
truth in these 'imitations' of life is part of their value, part of the
value of this phase of art. In judging such art from our later
point of vantage, with all the knowledge of later forms, and with
a keener sense of the complex structure and meanings of art-
works, we do not change all the criteria for judging the earlier
works. We do not say that some new criterion (expression, or
symbolic imagery, etc.) should displace the criterion of verisimilitude; we add the relevant later criteria to the still valid
criterion of verisimilitude as our understanding of the complexity of art deepens.

But in all this, one of the things art and literature have done is
to reveal, in a continuous creative discovery, how many variations the notion of verisimilitude, truth to appearance, general
likeness to nature, and so on, can sustain. As a result, the criterion remains alive and efficient, but not in a single or obvious
way. When we say that art 'discovers', and projects images of,
new aspects of the world and man, we are relying on the latent
possibilities of verisimilitude; we discover with each such
revelation of things not previously seen that way a new kind of
relationship between an art-image and the objects it represents;
and to declare this a new aspect, and therefore a discovery,
we have to refer this new art-image to the external world and
its objects. It is only when art and poetry present absolute
fantasy, or absolute expressionism, or an order of symbols

determined by specific ideas (as in some types of religious art) that the criterion of representational truth becomes inapplicable.

Thus the continuing interest of this criterion lies in the degree and manner of its applicability. Before considering a few prominent variations let us note that one does not need to think long before realizing that the problem of mimesis is linked from the start with that of sensation and perception. Sensations are not necessarily simple or clearly defined; and visual perceptions of objects occur without full visualization, or full realization of the objects as images. Every perception, and every image, depends on momentary isolation from the surrounding context and the continuum of sensation, as attention focuses on it; everything else is sacrificed at that moment. An art manipulates a medium—paint, stone, words, etc.—in such a way as to create images analogous to those derived from objects. Here we see that we already have two variables; one deriving from the focusing of attention on some things and not others, and the other resulting from the medium; images are isolated, and then transposed into, or invented by analogy in, a medium. The life we see in a play or a novel is like the life we see around us, without being it. It is an invention, using the same materials; perhaps like a wheel, the inventor of which took his wood from nature. The wheel is wood, but not a tree; it is a wheel. Poetic representations also have their double aspect. But literary art, which is an art of words, introduces another element of indirectness, as against painting and sculpture, because it is never the representation of specific people and things, in the sense of painters and their models, whether persons or objects. So the criterion we apply is rarely a simple: is the subject well portrayed? but something more intricate, such as: is the portrayal of life adequate enough, as a general analogy, to allow the interpretation to carry conviction? The good representation is both an analogy of real life, and an analogue of its interpretation, of seeing in a certain way.

Let us look at some variant possibilities. One of the clearest is the naturalistic style in the novel and drama towards the end of the nineteenth century. Clear, because in several important respects, in verbal description of characters and milieu, in dialogue, in the construction of plot and delineation of events, the most deliberate attempt was made to be realistically exact. A general purpose governed these particular aims; the interest lay in rejecting vulnerable idealism and romantic illusions, and revealing the harsh sides of life, and the cruel realities of human relations. To paint realities and not illusions—this was the burden of Strindberg and Ibsen, as it was of Zola's scientifically based determinism, and Hauptmann's portrayal of working-class conditions. Writers using this style made a gesture, saying: *this* is the truth of things, of men's lives, or their moral attitudes, or their biologically determined character. The response of the reader is to say: yes, you have shown me things that I know are the truth. In this creative aim and response mimesis and straight descriptive likeness are of the essence of the writing, and are criteria. They are so retrospectively. If this sort of literature proves to have permanent interest, beyond its original topical character, so that other aspects of value and criteria arise, these cannot negate the original intention and its corresponding criterion.

From the point of view of a comprehensive aesthetic the poetics of naturalism can easily be challenged. The famous formula of the German writer Arno Holz, summarizing a literary programme, was that the tendency of art was to revert to nature ('die Kunst hat die Tendenz, wieder Natur zu werden'). But one can argue that to make of art a replica of nature is impossible, even if desirable, so any representation must always be equivalent to the object minus some quantity owing to technical difficulties, and plus some other quantity of a subjective, selective, or interpretative kind. Nevertheless, the original intention, to be as near to reality in the mimesis as possible, remains valid. If you aim to be as naturalistic as possible, you will certainly be more so than if you aim at something less or different. In cases of this kind it is the *relative* degree of naturalism that counts.

A second prominent possibility of mimesis may be seen in art which presents ideal forms. In literature this appears as the portrayal, consciously pursued, of the 'universal', or 'general truth', in man and nature, examples of which are the practice of French classical authors, of the Augustans in England, and of Goethe and Schiller, in their classical phase, in Germany. The theoretical basis of ideal art is argued for painting in Reynolds's

Discourses, and for both art and literature in an important essay by Goethe, *Über die einfache Nachahmung der Natur, Manier, und Stil* (1788). Goethe distinguishes very clearly between the naturalism of simple figurative drawing; the mannerism of fantasy, the grotesque, and the distortions involved in intensely expressive or subjective art; and the ideal or typical or 'pure' forms which eliminate accident and present beauty and truth in a single image. This he calls 'style', giving the word an absolute meaning.

For the problem of mimesis as a criterion such a view, which is representative of a general trend in the eighteenth century in Europe, has a special interest, because it shows a creative relationship between object and subject. A selective factor is here at work which is not present in simple mimesis. The ideal-ist, or classical, artist believes it is possible to represent nature 'objectively'. He aims to distinguish the essential, or purest, or typical, forms of objects; but it is the object that he portrays, not fantasy or subjective feelings, like the romantics. Nevertheless he clearly makes a selection from the forms available; he in fact chooses the 'pure', essential ones; he makes his decision as to which of the forms he sees are the essentially true and typical ones, and which are accidental, local, and untypical, which are impure and distorted. Ideal art is thus constructive as well as mimetic; in a generalizing process ideal forms are constructed from the variety of real forms, and to do this is looked upon as the prime purpose of art. So clear an aim creates its own criter-ion. The reference to reality is essential. If you do not know that the forms are ideal, you do not know the meaning. This type of art must be judged as a statement of universalized, impersonal truth in the sensuous forms of fine art or the figurative forms of poetry.

A third example of variants of mimesis arises with impression-ism. Again we observe that a new mode of imitation is discover-ed, with the consequence that mimesis continues to be relevant as a criterion, but with an adjustment. The basic principle of the style is best understood, of course, from painting. Another way of interrupting the physical continuum, the flux of sensation, and fixing the resulting image, presents itself. Light is in this case all-important; that light which changes constantly, es-pecially in more northern countries. The impressionist painter painting a landscape looks not for its characteristic, typical, and constant general features, but for the relations of light and colour in their momentary immediacy. People often think, erroneously, that such painting is subjective; a mistake to be attributed to the popular, corrupt idea of impressionism, which takes the term to mean a rough, fleeting, imprecise 'impression' as against a studied and meditated representation. Impressionism, on the contrary, is an objective style, with nature as its object, seen however as light and colour rather than as outline and plastic form. And we might remind ourselves that it used the most rigorous and precise techniques to achieve its aim.

The criterion of verisimilitude is still applicable in such painting, in the sense that a particular landscape is referred to and the painting is of *that* one and not another. The style emerged in northern France, and not on the Mediterranean. When it first appeared it seemed strange, and many people failed to see the likeness to nature. They changed their minds when they realized that different aspects of the visual scene were being accentuated, with likeness still involved. In fact this change of style opened up enormously the possibilities of visual selection and emphasis, and the sense of the latent complexity of the visual world and its multifold presentation. We note then that, as with idealist art, there is a special object–subject relationship established. A constructive selection is exercised on objective nature, this time with the purpose of showing not an image of the unchanging essential features of objects or scenes, but one visual possibility out of many.

In its literary uses the term 'impressionism' has none of the technical precision it has for painting; it is vague and indeterminate. Above all, its meaning shifts decisively towards the subjective. In England it did not establish itself as a clear literary style. Some of Mallarmé's poetry suggests the trend, in the poetic aim to paint, not the object, but the effect it makes on the sensibility. More deliberate verbal impressionism was attempted by the German lyric poet Liliencron, and in prose writers like Schnitzler and early Thomas Mann it appears in conjunction with, or as a development of, naturalistic description. In fact the conscientious attempt at total naturalism, itself a more precise form of realism, leads inevitably to impressionism; that is, to the analytic breaking-down of the world of perception. In Hofmannsthal's early lyric dramas verbal impressionism informs the texture of lyrical monologues, but is also a consciously adopted theme, in the deliberate emphasis on transient and changing impressions of both external world and subjective feeling. The interest of this for our argument lies in the comparison with the idealist principle, and the adjustment of the criterion of likeness. The classical style presented the essential forms of nature; and though this, as we said, involves selection according to an idea, the result was believed to be basic, universally valid, objective truth. In impressionistic style, on the other hand, the basis is again truth, the truth of an object, but *one* truth, one aspect of its truth, one possibility, one latent thing brought to view, not a form believed to contain the absolute, purified, single quintessence of the object. But in both cases mimetic likeness is one of the valid criteria of judgement, because the reference to given objects provides the measure of significance.

The mimesis criterion ceases to function clearly in the symbolic and expressionist styles, artistic and literary, that follow impressionism. They are characterized by a frankly constructivist art which draws on images both from the outside world and from the inner world of memory, dream, fantasy, and the unconscious. The literary works evolved in this way, whether poems or fictions, are openly complex symbols which offer analogies, clue-signs, to inner experiences and states of consciousness. They are symbols either of the fusion of external and internal, of their interactions; or of purely internal events; but never of the external world alone, as in the case of naïve mimesis. This development, which was gradual and cumulative, may be followed in the European novel and drama since the turn of the century; in the point of view techniques of Henry James, in Proust's treatment of memory, in the double perspective of story and narrator created by Gide, in the interior monologue of Joyce, Virginia Woolf, and others, in the dream fantasies of Kafka, in Thomas Mann's ironical use of myth, parody, and montage, and in expressionist and symbolist drama. In each of these the simple mimetic has become entwined with complex reactions, and the exact relationship of inner and outer world, of mental experiences and their external

or internal motivation, has to be established each time differently by careful analysis.

In the development of expressionist and symbolistic styles the
representational factor, or mimesis, in its plainer forms has been
reduced. In novels and plays, however, it is difficult to eliminate
it altogether because the human person, even when used
abstractly, remains at the centre of the ideas or feelings presented, and it is difficult to see how this human centre can be
converted totally into abstract symbolism. The usual position
is that abstract, or symbolic, imagery is made to cohere round
a figure that is at the very least a schematic human person.
This is what happens in Beckett's plays, and, in a variant way,
in those of Ionesco. Beckett's plays are virtually static, but
potent, theatrical images of states of religious or philosophical
anxiety. The human figures in them are far removed from the
realistic round character; they have only a remnant of human
personality about them, being little more than tenuous signs for
generalizations. This is where mimesis ceases to be a criterion.
There are some people who would argue that works of this
kind are in fact 'representations' of feelings or states of emotion
or mind; it has been argued that lyric poems are 'representations of an action'. If this is true, one is still concerned with
mimesis. But a difficult problem of poetics is involved here. It
seems to me more practical to look on abstract style, and
symbolic imagery, in drama and fiction, as an instrument of
evocation; the images and image-patterns—of a Beckett play,
for example, or a Kafka novel—create analogies of mental
states or events rather than mimetic representations. But one
thing is worth noting. Verisimilitude is no longer applicable in
the mimetic sense; but something is carried over from it into
the assessment of these difficult styles. It is the sense that there is
a direct link between imagery and mental or emotional experience; that it is not simply abstract play, or a gymnastics of
fantasy, but is a sincere statement about human experience. In
such art mimetic truth is replaced as a criterion by the sense of a
'convincing' symbolism of the 'inner' world, a sense which must
rest on the conscious or unconscious recognition of subtle,
oblique references to one's own inner experiences. In other
words a different kind of corroboration is substituted for that of
simple, naturalistic representation.

9

IDEAS, BELIEFS, AND
PHILOSOPHICAL AWARENESS

IN the first part of this book the questions of subject and thought
were discussed and their importance reaffirmed. In this place
we look at the problem of thought in literary works from the
point of view of evaluation. Stated simply, the questions most
frequently put run: must literary works, to be important, have
a content of ideas? Ought they normally to offer some view of
life, some *Weltanschauung* or philosophy?

A beginning is often made by writers on this topic by referring
to the famous dictum of Mallarmé that poetry is made not of
ideas but of words. It was at the time a revolutionary utterance,
introducing a new programme. Nowadays everyone accepts it,
so there is no harm in saying that the point is too obvious and
easy in respect of lyric poetry, especially in its highly specialized
and *recherché* forms, in which sound, rhythm, figures of speech,
and verbal interaction are so prominently part of the meaning.
But what is a novel made of, or a drama? Though they too are
made of words, their verbal character is very different, and the
contextual elements, the intralinguistic evocations, are quite
different in kind, function, and intensity. The scale of operation
is broader, the textures more open-meshed; one cannot simply
say: is the art in the words? Since I want to consider the
problem on a wider base than lyric alone, I must put the
question rather differently. What we will ask is not: do novels
and plays state ideas or thoughts directly, discursively—
but: is a given novel or play a medium in which ideas
are implicit? Does it convey indirectly an attitude to life,
a philosophy, a set of values, etc. etc.? In this sense such
works do contain serious statements about life, but expressed in
an oblique, or analogical way. This is the true criterion enabling
us to distinguish an important and sincere work from a trivial
one.

Of one thing we ought to be clear at the outset. It may be

customary nowadays for poetics to play down heavily the thought-content of poems; nevertheless, some kinds of didactic poetry in the past set out deliberately to embody ideas, and if the latter are extracted from such work what is left can be very exiguous. In the ode form thoughts, sentences, and near-discursive statements are everywhere in evidence. In the eighteenth century, again, a common attitude was to compose a philosophical poem in which a common stock of ideas were presented in 'poetic form', or 'adorned by poetry', and presumably the ideas were felt to be part of the value for money, or of the total experience, as we should probably say now. Didactic poetry has to be appreciated as such, and not as though it were romantic *Erlebnislyrik* or a bit of Mallarmean symbolism.

In a way, of course, it is a pointless question. The fact is that in genius, as in nature and human character, everything is possible, any and every combination of interests and gifts. The result is that when a man with the gift of verse- (or drama-, or fiction-) making is also interested in philosophical ideas, he inevitably runs the two together and philosophical poetry emerges; and we can add that his ideas can be either his own, or derivative, or a mixture of both. This is what all philosophical poetry is. It is an amalgam, but a unity, an indivisible kind, that we must accept; all attempts to put the significance into the poetic, or aesthetic, component alone are beside the point.

Another essentially straightforward case that is obscured by misdirected questions is that of parable, and fable, which we have already touched on above. The moral of such poems is often a commonplace, for which reason a pure-grained aesthete regards only the treatment as having poetic value. But this breaks open the unity of meaning; it suggests that the poem is moving in two directions at once, one valuable, the other not; whereas the treatment, or poetic form, is in fact a presentation of the didactic meaning. Separating the two is to shift the significance from the whole poem to one of its parts.

Bernard Shaw, who wrote parables in dramatic form, was very sensible about this point. Artists only attracted his interest if they had a philosophy, as for instance Michelangelo, John Bunyan, Goethe, Wagner, and Ibsen had. He believed in parable, and art was most significant for him when it consisted of parables. His own plays belong to this category, and we remember how he disparaged Shakespeare for having no philosophy but merely expressing commonplaces about life that everyone knows for himself after a few years of adult experience. This attitude is probably shared by large numbers of people—'I like a play with ideas in it', 'I like a novel that gives you something to think about'. And it may be that professional students of literature underestimate its potency and influence, and moreover its legitimacy. Literature may not be just direct moral teaching, but no one can forbid it to have relations with morals, whether of individuals or societies; or, nowadays, with scientific thought and world-views which influence culture and social institutions. It seems to me, for instance, that Brecht's impact is due largely to his moral fervour. His apologists tell us vociferously that he is of course not only a doctrinaire but a poet. It may be true. But quite apart from the element of doctrinaire politics Brecht has played variations on two great themes— poverty and peace, or money and war—which are central problems of world life in our age and time. Without this substance his notorious theatrical experiments would be hollow.

In spite of Shaw's clear position there are people who try to detach a literary phenomenon, which they call Shaw's 'comic fantasy', from the socialist ideology, to which they are indifferent. Certainly the fact that one can sit in the theatre and laugh heartily at a Shaw play without being remotely a socialist does lend plausibility to the disruption of idea and form here effected, and one can forgive anyone for slipping too carelessly into the belief that the ideas don't matter. To do this, however, would be to admire a mechanism in the abstract, or simply to enjoy superficial comic detail, and thereby fail to make a proper judgement. The reference to ideas in Shaw is in reality an essential criterion in understanding and judging the comedy; for he bases this latter on characters placed in situations which reveal their socio-political prejudices and inconsistencies of attitude in farcical consequences. Without social class and snobbery there is no comedy in *Pygmalion*.

In T. S. Eliot, who was as firmly anchored in Christian philosophy as Shaw in his mixture of Lamarck and socialism, we find another slant on this problem. Eliot has a highly developed sense of the differing functions of poetry and philosophical beliefs. It appears sharply in his rejection of the claim of poetry since the romantic period to be a substitute for religion. Eliot looks for his philosophy and theology in the relevant sources. Poetry does not exist to do their job, but one of its own, for which reason alone we cultivate it. It is a mistake, he believes, to ask poetry to do more than its own task or give more than it can. Moreover, if we do not expect poetry to create philosophies or religions we shall be able to enjoy it all the more as poetry.

This is interesting because it shows Eliot opposed to an empty or effete aestheticism, and to the dogma of absolute poetry, and equally opposed to agnostics and sceptics. He sees poetry naturally linked with belief and philosophy, but supplementing and enriching them, not trying mistakenly to initiate or replace them. This implies, it seems to me, a belief that poetry expresses the *emotional* or existential context of belief and philosophy, and in this way adds something of its own; and secondly, it suggests a ritualistic function which also belongs organically to the context of religious ideas.

An inescapable problem arises of course in the question as to whether, given an underlying philosophy, we evaluate this philosophy separately *per se* when we evaluate the poetry that is in some way its vehicle. I have referred to this problem in Part I in connection with the role of sympathy in making judgements. In practice it seems to me that we do evaluate the ideas; we do so by acceptance or qualified acceptance, or plain rejection; and it is my contention that these qualifications do reduce the value of our judgements of works as meaningful wholes. It leads to what I have called partial judgements. Many think otherwise. They hold that one can allow for an unacceptable philosophy and still make a valid judgement of the poetry. One might concede that with works involving beliefs of a more dogmatic kind an equalizing factor is that the same, or at least a similar, emotional framework underlies differing beliefs; one can for instance respond to the religious plays of Claudel or Eliot so long as one feels involved with evil, remorse, and the need for a purification or liberation from guilt, though one may not accept the Christian terms for these problems.

Eliot's position on this matter is in fact helpful. His adverse estimate of Shelley is well known.[1] It is based on the view that Shelley's philosophy was immature, and incapable of deserving one's respect. This is Eliot's yardstick in the difficult matter of judging when one does not share the beliefs or philosophy expressed. Where this is the case the lack of assent does not matter so long as the philosophical ideas of the poem 'correspond to some large area of human experience', by virtue of which they are 'tenable', seen to be a possibility and therefore commanding respect. Such was the Senecan philosophy favoured by some Renaissance writers. Under these conditions it is possible to assess and accept a poem of different philosophical colour from one's own beliefs. But an imperfect, or insufficiently worked out philosophy can only have an adverse effect on a poem and lead to a negative judgement. There is no doubt here that an evaluation of the ideas precedes or accompanies that of the poetic expression. The principle can be extended on the one hand to any of the incidental ideas or beliefs or attitudes in a work, for clearly authors do not necessarily imply in all their works, and some authors perhaps not in any, a single, profound, all-comprehending philosophical basis; and on the other a point is reached where the *range* of philosophical or ethical sensitiveness enters into the evaluation of an author, as one sees by juxtaposing Molière and Maupassant, or Yeats and Rossetti, or Ibsen and Synge.

Going a step further we remember that the problem is not always posed in the relatively simple terms so far noted, as one of a given philosophy within the framework of which poems are written. Things are still clear in religious poetry; in Donne, Herbert, Vaughan, or the German baroque poets. But in most works, including the novel and drama, we are dealing not with a systematic philosophy, not with one of the well-established pagan or Christian systems, but with very varying, individualized patterns of belief or values, and often with a deliberate avoidance of system, dogma, or consistent doctrine. For this reason I suggest the term 'philosophical awareness' as the quality that must be present if works are not to be trivial, or superficial, or simply mechanical story-writing or versifying. In every work that claims literary rank we should be able to feel a latent philosophical power, an awareness of philosophical

[1] *The Use of Poetry and the Use of Criticism* (London, 1933), chapter V.

values, an undertone of secret intuitive knowledge of, or wisdom about, human things. This is the unsystematic counterpart in unorthodox writers to doctrine in writers like Milton and Eliot and Claudel. For though doctrine does not make poetry, poetry is not poetry if it remains at the trivial, unimportant level. One can put this another way by saying that one must be able to discern in a literary book, under the surface, between the lines, in the configuration of plot and characters, in the imagery, the sort of ideas or thoughts that otherwise make up the subject-matter of serious thought about life and human beings. Most people, the sub-intelligent and the feckless excepted, have to confront life; they are forced to think about their situation, character, desires, actions; and in consequence there are in everyone the germs of that sustained thought that is expressed in intense forms in philosophy, religion, ethics, and social philosophy. The poet, the novelist, thinks concretely, in images, and the joining of imagination to his philosophical or ethical insights makes him acceptable to intelligent, thinking people who by passive imagination are responsive to his mode of statement; and, beyond that, the exercise of poetry, as of all art, shows it as a device by which alone certain areas of knowledge, experience, and truth can be demonstrated. The imagination, the thought, the device go together, and hence the quality of thought, of latent or implicit philosophy—which includes beliefs and sense of values—belongs to the primary criteria of a literary work.

Whether such awareness remains implicit, or whether it crystallizes to some extent into explicit didactic statement, depends on the temperament and style of the author. The Shavian favourites listed above show a fair measure of combined explicit and implicit; symbolist poems, on the other hand, ply the implicit to the point of obscurity. But it should be emphasized that *thought* is involved, and not only feeling. The aesthetic that shifts the significance, and the special function, of poetry, simply into 'feeling' and its expression is inadequate; it misses the peculiar mystery of the marriage between thought and feeling that is consummated in the device of symbolic language and imagery. Ideas are presented in terms of sensibility, thought suspended in a context of story, captured in symbols, half shrouded, half emergent. A cogent schematic example appears in Thomas Mann's early stories, which show him indecisively hovering between two incompatible philosophers, Schopenhauer and Nietzsche. The latter, in philosophical argument, draw conclusions of *thought* about the primacy of mind (*Geist*) or life; Schopenhauer in the metaphysical opposition of the 'will' (life) and idea (mind), with precedence given to mind; Nietzsche, on the other hand, giving precedence to the life-values against the failure of the will-to-live observable in decadent philosophies. Thomas Mann, not a professional philosopher, but philosophically sensitive, projects this conflict of values into contrasting character types, like the cultured, artistic, but consumptive Frau Klöterjahn, and her brawny, vigorous, and aggressive, but intellectually mediocre husband, in the story *Tristan*. Mann, as novelist, gives a picture of life and temperaments that express the conflict of ideas as a matter of felt values and attitudes; and the objective clash of characters reflects the subjective conflict in himself. A more intricate, but equally cogent example may be found in Chekhov's plays. They are impregnated with social analysis, but it is expressed indirectly in terms of suffering characters and their feelings, in their frustrations and distress. He shows us through these persons the malaise experienced by a whole social class, Russian bourgeois society, at the beginning of this century. Another striking example, moreover, is tragedy, as a genre. All tragedy contains a judgement on human life in its relation to non-human or supra-human powers, agencies, or beings. It is a challenge to the gods; it is a moral indictment; it puts a question-mark against human life in its confusion and conflict. These are not questions of pure 'aesthetis'. The meaning of tragedy can never reside in the aesthetic–poetic alone.

The criterion of thought just expounded is one of the most misunderstood, because it is mistakenly seen as a wedge that prises apart the wholeness, the indivisibility and autonomous character of a work. It is often said in consequence that the meaning is not in any thought or thoughts or philosophy, and so on, but 'in the poetry', in 'the work itself as verbal art', 'in the words', which in fact affirms an autotelic and esoteric object sealed off, if we are quite logical, from comment or interpretation. The better way to view this problem in my view is, as I suggested in Part I, to see the reader in a parallel relationship to the writer. Just as the latter experiences his philosophy, beliefs, values, his truth, by intuition working on nature and men, and creates in his medium an analogy for this, so the reader responds with the same double interest; he is attracted equally by the content, by the mode of the experiencing and and the thinking, and by the medium used for the analogy. He likes *this way* of thinking about life, and becoming more fully conscious of it. He likes to be *shown* truths, interpretations, and documents of things, to be led to them through story, through images, and through the complex language and music of lyric. But still he likes what he is led to; he would be quickly bored of enjoying sensuous surfaces, or imagery, or plots, or the art, if they were vacuous and trivial, and not the instruments of important meanings.

This is perhaps the point where we must admit, however enthusiastic we may be about medium, and the symbolism of forms and images as the central area of specifically aesthetic or poetic meaning, that spirituality is an ultimate value of all art, and that it transcends its location in a phenomenal form, the sensuous medium and symbolism. It appears through art, and so the art is important; but the art is not the identity of the spiritual. There is a value, and an experience of it, that joins Shakespeare, Michelangelo, and Bach behind and beyond their media, their modes of symbolism. And this, in its turn, joins devotees of various arts to numerous artists, and different kinds of artist, in spite of the art and medium. It is their spirituality we understand, even though we do not enter completely into all their sensuous modes, or their specific philosophical attitudes. Of these we choose our own; but, as we argued above, we are curious about others.

It is a corollary that art is valid as a *universal* public possession by virtue of its spirituality. Its individualization occurs through its media, and each of these restricts its audience, just as philosophy, value-systems, credos, and also taste, do. All modern insistence on the art-ness of art, the words-syndrome of poetry, the medium and craft aspects, the otherness of sensuous media transformed into symbolism, all this does justice to important individual variations of art, but it restricts the audience; by insisting on the mystery of the integrated art form or symbol as a hermetic meaning it excludes some of the possibilities of human communication and participation. Conversely, to stress the spirituality of art against medium widens its range of significance in and for the experience of a more universal public. These two tendencies have to be taken together: they both belong to the experience of art and literature.

In the highly individualized literature of the post-Renaissance centuries there is of course a very great range of beliefs and philosophical foundations, of individual intuitional experience or vision, and systems of values; in other words, an enormous differentiation of what I have called philosophical sensitiveness. The general development has been accompanied by a good deal of scepticism about general principles, with the result that it is by now much commoner to find in literary works a sensitive exploration of truth and values than any direct affirmation of particular truths or values. Much art has become the main instrument of agnostic groping and testing, or, when it is not this, the vehicle of emotional states, precise or imprecise, or loosely attached to large clues like alienation, or exile, or nihilism, or loss of identity, and the like.

What has to be made clear at this point of my argument is that the criterion of philosophical import is wholly clear when a recognizable philosophy is involved, and when judgement *must* take account of how this particular philosophy is handled (Christian allegory, Milton, rationalist fable and satire, romantic reflective poetry, etc. etc.); but much less obviously clear where individual values are concerned, or where the emphasis is on the exploration of the human situation, or where the motive for writing is principally emotional expression, or where, as is claimed nowadays, new emotions are created by the manipulation of the medium. The criterion then comes to rely on the sense of truth in the work; this must be convincing, as critics commonly say, conveying with this phrase acceptance of something as sincere and true; its opposite, the not being convinced, occurs when a work shows symptoms of falsity, frivolity, or dishonesty.

This is where the criterion becomes intricate, and hard to explain, although in fact critics work all the time with the notion of the convincing—it must be one of the most tired words of criticism today, for it is constantly used where conviction is most difficult. It is intricate because it cannot rest on a point-to-point reference between a work's details and possible models from life outside; one only needs to recall Kafka or Beckett to realize this. But it may only be due to the fact that we know so little about some kinds of mental process—the chemistry and physiology of thinking and imagining are, after all, as complex as of the body; in the physical area vast amounts remain to be discovered, whilst in the mental area we still rely almost entirely on our unconscious and unanalysed mechanisms. The sense of conviction can only rest on an elaborate system of signs in the responses and reactions of thought, consciousness, imagination, and memory to a literary work; in the evocation in the work of patterns overlapping with numerous patterns from our own experience and knowledge, which are seen to connect and relate; so that between the signs of the work and the responding patterns in the mind a set of connections is created which we then call a convincing meaning. When these processes fail or are obstructed we say the work does not carry conviction; it is incomplete, distorted, false, not credible.

Summarizing, we may say that this criterion—whether a work should have a factor of serious thought—is indeed valid, though it applies in different ways according to the kind of literature. Broadly speaking, we note four large categories of application: (1) straight philosophical poetry; (2) fable and parable; either direct, in the genres of the same name, or oblique, in fictions and plays that illustrate given values; a vast amount of literature is oblique parable in this sense (comedy, for instance, or eighteenth-century novels); (3) the literature of inquiry, the analysis, discovery, and clarification of experience and ideas; (4) 'expressionist' and symbolist literature, which give analogues of emotional truth or of non-logical intuitions of a metaphysical kind, and which are the most difficult of all to assess.

As a pendant to this section let us consider briefly the question whether a thought, an idea, can of itself be poetic. I do not refer to the phenomenon common in romantic poetry and theory, whereby certain things—like the past, or love, or the Crusades, or the Church—could be designated poetic; or whereby one could see the ultimate goal of man and nature as a transformation into poetry (a dream of Novalis). What I mean is not dependent on a particular *Weltanschauung*, nor on symbolic or analogical notions, but appears in such lines and phrases as:

> Men must endure
> Their going hence, even as their coming hither:
> Ripeness is all.

> Tel qu'en Lui-même enfin l'éternité le change.

> Alles Vergängliche ist nur ein Gleichnis.

> Ein Rätsel ist Reinentsprungenes.

None of these statements is of the lyric–poetic type, expressing feeling in song, although two are from lyric poems, and the third from the closing chorus of *Faust*. They are all statements of a thought, and in my view this thought strikes one as the important thing, and is a powerful focus of attention. And even though feeling is generated it gathers round the thought-centre and supports it, but without replacing or changing it, or diminishing its luminosity, or its thought-quality. One notices, too, the absence of metaphor, except in the Shakespeare, and even here ripeness is not a full metaphor but hovers between the figurative and the literal. The Goethe is interesting, because the thought, which is sublime, calls attention to similes, analogies, but none is used in the formulation. In none of these is the keen poetic impression evoked by blatantly figurative language, nor by spurts of feeling. The paradox (which is a trope) in Baudelaire's line is effective. But of usual poetic means it is the rhythm that effects most; each passage, brief as it is, has a beautiful dignity, perhaps allied to resignation, in its movement. The Hölderlin line proves on inspection to be a highly organized phonetic pattern, and the compound *Reinentsprungenes*, a nominalization of a past participle fused with an initial adverb, is a wonderful creation. But when these features have been allowed for it is the thought itself that is written big. They are examples of imagination creating thought. It is not here symbolization that is involved, or expressive imagery, to mention two of the commonest and most accepted poetic principles. Elsewhere in poetry the imagination is applied to the presentation of subjects and ideas, working obliquely with a wealth of images. The imagination shows the thought. Here the thought itself is so designed that it shows its origin in the imagination.

Piety, religious feeling, the suggestions of a high wisdom to be attained by mortals, the sense of the numinous—these do provide, of course, a vast emotional envelope for such oracular thoughts, and perhaps they implement the special poetry of these lines. Nevertheless, in the centre are thoughts, *these thoughts*, as quite precise statements; they are in no way large gestures or woolly invocations, or simple emotional expressions.

Some *pensées* of Pascal are related to this phenomenon, and one can observe a process whereby a statement initially set out as prose shifts into a poetic mode. Thus, for example, the famous: 'Le silence éternel de ces espaces infinies m'effraie.' Here the thought of the unbroken silence in the cosmos is extremely impressive. And it *is* a thought. T. S. Eliot has pointed out that Pascal is not referring superficially to the sense of magnitude, or boundless space, but to the silence, which is the cause of his anxiety. Even more than in the quoted passages, however, this initially prose thought is suffused with emotion, and developed towards an emotional climax. Finally, in this case, a dramatic–expressive utterance overlays the *pensée*, the thought.

10

METAPHORICAL UNITY

THAT a work should have unity, or aim to effect a unity of impression, is a commonplace of criticism. The negatives are frequently heard: it is a play that falls to pieces, a rambling, aimless novel, a badly composed poem. Simple ideas of unity are not enough, however, to cover what is involved in literary works. Often the term 'organic unity' is used, which suggests a unity arising from functional relationships; it is a better term, though more analogy than definition.

Unity is, of course, essential to any statement of meaning. The parts of a statement are disposed in such a way as to form a focus, at which the meaning appears; and this applies to single sentences, or to paragraphs, or to long, complex statements. Unity here is a common-sense notion of order; it is instrumental unity, appearing in the controlled direction of the thoughts, in congruent pointers, in proper subordination and sequence.

This kind of unity is not an exclusive feature, or criterion, of art. Let us call it architectonic, or compositional, unity; it concerns structure, but in an external, not an expressive, sense. It is a feature of many things that are not art or poetry; of a machine, a company report, a trial, a town plan, the procedure of a meeting, and so on; and it would be merely casuistical to argue that these things become art when they show a good, orderly shape. The sense of order, of subordination of parts, of sequence, do belong to some aesthetic effects, but they are features of many kinds of rationalization and organization, of hierarchies, institutions, and formal arrangements that are often called empty or soulless and are the antithesis of the animated forms of art. In fact, a very common feature of low-category literary works is an excellent architectonic plan. The most unpretentious magazine romances are well-constructed. Indeed, the craft of writing them is learned in a hard school, and we scholars who pass them by forget that often as much craft and skill goes to their making as does to that of good literature.

Detective novels are a good example of compositional unity. Their form is basically a riddle, the material being economically organized in strict relationship to a central mystery, which inevitably yields architectonic unity and even formal beauty.

As a descriptive term, with an implied basis of judgement, 'organic unity' comes much nearer to the nature of the work of art[1]. It indicates functional structure; that the parts or elements of a whole organism are adapted to each other, and to the whole, and are in harmony. Thus, in a poem, the metre and imagery are appropriate to the feelings or ideas or incidents, and no details are included that do not contribute in some way to the whole. 'Organic' is, of course, a metaphor as applied to a constructed thing like a work of art; a picture, or a poem, are not strictly speaking organisms, because they do not live, grow, and die as organisms do. Since, however, in the manner of their genesis, and sometimes slowish progress towards their final form, unconscious processes of nature are involved, and a waiting on moments of inspired synthesis, there is perhaps an element of reality as well as of metaphor in this term 'organic unity', if art-works are seen as human creations.

But terms like 'functional' and 'organic', helpful though they are, do not describe the particular specific characteristic of literary works; this is unity of texture, fusing with the larger unity of composition, and one needs the notions of analogy, congruence, and even metaphor, to evoke the pattern that can act as a touchstone. For in this complex unity not only different elements, but a group of essential elements, are concerned. Put briefly, they are a subject-matter, which may be story or ideas; the feelings and emotions associated with them; the imagery; and language itself, the vehicle of everything. The ways in which these interact differ with the form; in lyric poetry the texture is close-knit, in the novel looser, whilst drama is varied according to the kind and to the use of prose or verse. But the essential process is the same. These elements interact in such a way that they may be said to take on mutually something of each other's character; they are modified, and adapted towards each other. Ideas become charged with emotion, and associated

---

[1] My argument is independent, but I would like to recommend the important article by Catherine Lord on this subject, 'Organic Unity Reconsidered', in *Aesthetic Inquiry*, ed. M. C. Beardsley and H. M. Schueller (Belmont, Calif., 1967), pp. 82–89.

with images. Feelings are expressed in symbols, or symbolical persons, and are thus transmuted into ideas, or ideal forms. Images become, in association with an evolving total meaning, a kind of thought, as do persons and events. Language is exploited in its sensuous, evocative, auditory, and imaginal properties, so that it loses its defining quality and becomes a kind of imagery. By unity in literary art we mean the harmonious meaning or effect arising from the interaction and mutual modification of these diverse elements. It is within this unity, which rests on analogical congruence of elements, and is far more subtle than external, large-scale, compositional unity, that language ceases to be practical or conceptual and instead is used to make symbolic or metaphorical textures. This process, whereby meaning is suspended in a complex structure of language *and* imagery, is a principal criterion of literary art.

It is the factor of analogy that suggests the term 'metaphorical unity' for this phenomenon. Metaphor rests on analogies, and uses sensuous images to point meanings. This it does even in common language, with its wealth of outworn, or faded, metaphors. In poetry it goes beyond plain, illustrative use. Take any example from Shakespeare:

> When in the chronicle of wasted time
> I see descriptions of the fairest wights . . .

> Since I left you mine eye is in my mind,
> And that which governs me to go about
> Doth part his function and is partly blind . . .

King Richard: Why, uncle, thou hast many years to live.
Gaunt: But not a minute, king, that thou canst give:
> Shorten my days thou canst with sullen sorrow,
> And pluck nights from me, but not lend a morrow;
> Thou canst help time to furrow me with age,
> But stop no wrinkle in his pilgrimage;
> Thy word is current with him for my death,
> But dead, thy kingdom cannot buy my breath.

Here one sees how the explanatory function of making the sense clear is accompanied by a doubling and redoubling of sensuous vividness; a vitality and richness develop in the picture or statement which not only clarify but enhance the situation and its attendant feeling. In other words the metaphor not only serves the meaning, by clearly illustrating it, but it establishes or helps to create the representation as a whole, and to express the emotions involved. It goes far beyond showing 'the unity of things', or unexpected resemblances, or being an ornament.

Metaphor is of the very essence of poetic creation because reason and imagination work together to produce it. It combines very disparate things: thought and sensuous image, abstract and concrete, insight and emotion; it is both heightened meaning and heightened evocation of the world, man, and his feelings. It is a synthesizing power, in contrast to the separative, analytic functions of other modes of language; it expresses several aspects of the mind instead of one. It expresses a subtle *interfusion* of thoughts, vision, and feelings. In addition, it is a natural language of passion and strong feeling, which normally seek an outlet in hyperbolic, figurative language. In metaphor all these things are fused, and they are so at the very roots of expression, as the metaphor springs to the mind in a single inspiration and as immediate synthesis. Its unity is an interfusion and a congruence of insight, image, meaning, expressive effect, and expressive relief, secured at a stroke. This is the kind of unity present in all poetic composition, for which reason metaphor is in itself a model of literary art in general. Hence we add the term 'metaphorical unity' to the commoner notion of architectonic unity, and as a more precise term than the analogical organic unity. This conception is also more illuminating about poetic forms than the blanket term 'symbolic' so much used in recent decades, especially in the wake of Susanne Langer's books on aesthetics. The idea of metaphor covers more effectively the essential semantic element in literary art, because metaphor always combines a semantic clue with symbolising imagery. A pattern of untied symbols, or symbol-images, is in essence a dream, or an expression equivalent to unconscious or trance activity. But a symbol with a clue combines semantic and symbolic to give the consciously perfected poetic statement.

This kind of unity is one of *texture*, of the fabric itself, and not only of the total design. This feature is apparent in any section of a literary work, in a single verse, in a paragraph, in a passage of dialogue. An important consequence is that our judgement of literary quality is based in the first place on the texture, not on a work in its totality. Take the following passages:

Sweet day, so cool, so calm, so bright,
The bridall of the earth and skie . . .

Turning and turning in the widening gyre
The falcon cannot hear the falconer . . .

From leaf to leaf in silence
The year's new green
Is passed along northward . . .

When to the sessions of sweet silent thought . . .

Der abend wiegte schon die Erde . . .

These are all fragments, beginnings of poems, and uncompleted
thoughts. There can be no question of judging a 'total unity',
since the poem is only just starting; but the poetic mode is
unmistakable. The same process appears in the other arts. We
do not need a whole canvas to recognize artistic quality. We
can tell it from any section of a painting, just as we can
recognize quality in a pianist from the first bars he plays,
without having to wait until he has played right through his
piece.

We observe this unity of texture in prose, too, though it is
not so intense as in poetry. Obviously one could quote from
any masterpiece of fiction, but a relatively modest and less
well-known passage from Hardy will serve as illustration, the
beginning of the story *A Tragedy of Two Ambitions:*

The shouts of the village-boys came in at the window, accompanied
by broken laughter from loungers at the inn-door; but the brothers
Halborough worked on.

They were sitting in a bedroom of the master-millwright's house,
engaged in the untutored reading of Greek and Latin. It was no
tale of Homeric blows and knocks, Argonautic voyaging or Theban
family woe that inflamed their imaginations and spurred them on-
ward. They were plodding away at the Greek Testament, immersed
in a chapter of the idiomatic and difficult Epistle to the Hebrews.

The Dog-day sun in its decline reached the low ceiling with
slanting sides, and the shadows of the great goat's-willow swayed and
interchanged upon the walls like a spectral army manœuvring.
The open casement which admitted the remoter sounds now brought
the voice of some one close at hand. It was their sister, a pretty girl
of fourteen, who stood in the court below.

'I can see the tops of your heads! What's the use of staying up there? I like you not to go out with the street-boys; but do come and play with me!'

They treated her as an inadequate interlocutor, and put her off with some slight word. She went away disappointed.

This passage shows in an easy, simple way what one can expect from good narrative writing. A picture of character, place, thing, situation, is projected; it creates an effect, of drama, atmosphere, mystery, expectancy, and so on, arresting the attention; it plays usually on feelings or emotion; it rouses the mind and the judgement, and the sense of significance, values, qualities; it appeals to the sense of life and the sense of truth, in one gesture; and it is round and full, not by simple accumulation of a mass of dull detail, but by a complex effect in which all these things interfuse in a unified, harmonious way. Conversely the writing is poor, faulty, or unliterary, when any of these elements are lacking or disturbed; that is, when the verbal evocation is unclear, or false; when the effect is, if present at all, too facile or stagey; when the emotional appeal is sentimental or banal; when the projection is lifeless, and the whole conventional, commonplace, and disjointed.

In prose there is a vastly greater range of styles, of intensities, and of the mixture of imaginative elements, so that it is often not possible to come so quickly to the judgement of quality as with verse. There is also a large area of fiction, particularly of mystery and crime fiction, and also of good middlebrow novels, where the writing is efficient and businesslike; it can then pass for a type of literary skill, rising superior to commonplace or bad story-writing, without achieving the synthesis of qualities that is the mark of fine imagination in narrative.

In thus stressing the nature of 'metaphorical' unity in texture I do not wish to reduce the importance of overall, or compositional, unity; far from it. Nor is every single bit of every work, even of verse, always as decisive as the verse examples quoted above. But a clear implication of the view put forward is that judging literary art, or art quality, is not the same thing as judging a work in its totality. Indeed we see at this point a significant feature in the whole process of judging and evaluating. They are always progressive; not single intuitive acts, as is so readily imagined, but a sequence of numerous impressions and judgements, of expanded, revised and recapitulated judgements, proceeding from parts to whole. As one reads, a provisional sense of quality attaches one to the book or poem, and from then on the process of evaluation is continuous.

On the recognition of 'metaphorical' unity, as against compositional, depends, too, the judgement of fragments and unfinished work, of which the Sapphic fragments, or Hölderlin's late poetic drafts, are examples. It helps, too, with the evaluation of all the excellent and fluent, but careless poets, like Byron, who write inspired passages and jingles by turns. Or again, one may observe convincing quality in the texture, whilst finding it difficult to perceive a perfect carrying-through of unity in a whole work.[1] And indeed, how many novels are really and truly unified economies, in the strictest sense of perfect inter-relationship of all the parts, with nothing superfluous and no loose ends? For every perfect novel there are a thousand perfect chapters. Still another example would be the plays of Goethe, including *Faust*, where, in the face of sheer abundance and diversity of motifs, the strict test of essentially dramatic unity breaks down.

Conversely, the sense of textures enables us to see when a work is unsatisfactory in spite of having a good compositional shape. A number of conventional forms illustrate the point, because they have an inherent power, beauty, or expressiveness, which is the very reason why they stay alive instead of being displaced by new inventions. The sonnet is an example; its abstract form has a beauty which appears even amidst the wreckage or banality of bad words. Formal effectiveness results also from the short-story form based on the final dramatic pointing or illumination, and its virtue is felt, as in the case of the sonnet, even where the contents of the story are trivial or facile, as in the weaker stories of Maupassant, Maugham, or Greene. An example from the dramatic genre is the scheme of the well-made play, which is a formal crystallization of essential dramatic crisis situations.

An example from lyric poetry of disjunction between a reasonably promising metrical–musical compositional form and a

---

[1] An example of this difficulty is discussed in Cleanth Brooks's article about Joyce's *Ulysses*, in *Imagined Worlds*, ed. M. Mack and I. Gregor (London, 1968), pp. 419 ff.

verbal texture otherwise poor would in my opinion be Matthew
Arnold's *Requiescat*, to take a harmless example from long ago.

> Strew on her roses, roses,
>   And never a spray of yew.
> In quiet she reposes;
>   Ah! would that I did too.
>
> Her mirth the world required;
>   She bathed it in smiles of glee.
> But her heart was tired, tired,
>   And now they let her be.
>
> Her life was turning, turning,
>   In mazes of heat and sound;
> But for peace her soul was yearning,
>   And now peace laps her round.
>
> Her cabin'd, ample spirit,
>   It flutter'd and fail'd for breath;
> To-night it doth inherit
>   The vasty hall of death.

Poor diction, trite, weak, inadequate metaphors, bathos,
sentimental ideas, and flat effects, make this poem unbearable,
though it was an anthology piece for many decades. But in spite
of these faults of texture, the metrical handling and the
consistent composition, based through the four stanzas on a
single contrast of emotional appearances and emotional
reality, provide the framework for a grave and sad poem that
never shakes itself free into true verbal form.

The point need not be laboured further. Judgement of
textural quality, and of a total work, are separate aspects of
evaluation, though they are complementary. But metaphorical
unity of texture is the more important. For if the fault is
architectonic and not textural we speak only of relative failure,
failure to sustain the quality throughout a whole. But if the
texture is poor no amount of abstract compositional unity can
make a complete poetic reality. One can only see in the shadows
an outline that has not been filled in.

11

NOVELTY

Whether works must be original in ideas and form, whether they must show striking novelty, is another of the most frequently posed questions and the most often misunderstood. Nowadays, after a good spate of experimentation and new styles in all the arts, and in a climate of continuing revolt-mindedness, which is threatening to become as established as the establishment, the idea that art should offer something new is more likely to be acceptable than not. But it is also prone to degenerate into an uncritical desire for mere new fashions.

Nevertheless, there is no doubt that new art has often been rejected, one reason at least being its unfamiliarity. It seems to be a permanent feature of the public relations of the arts, particularly since the eighteenth century. Perhaps we should not attach too much blame to caution; if very serious values are embodied in art-works we can be excused, having once recognized and enjoyed them, for thinking that they may probably recur in similar forms, or that we might like them to, on the principle of known delights.

Three notions especially have a bearing on this: universality, tradition, and the idea of classics and classical. They are in practice strong conservative influences, though there is no good theoretical reason why they should be. The criterion of universality dies hard. Perhaps it needn't disappear altogether, but it certainly should be redefined. What does a good novel or play do? 'They say something *universally* true about life.' There seems to be a strong urge to require of books the widest possible reference, or degree of generalization, and indeed to reserve for the general alone the name of truth, denying it to the local or temporary, which is degraded to a kind of unreality and non-existence. The idea goes hand in hand with the 'classical', and with the criterion of 'permanence', generating an aim for literature, that it should try to portray permanent truths, which can best be done by avoiding certain things—the topical, the contemporary, the local, the here-and-now. Good literature is thus timeless, so the argument runs, and will obviously tend to have a timeless family resemblance look about it, which is the aura of 'the classics'. Will it be read in ten years' time? is a frequent comment.

In the present age, it is true, we speak more usually of images and symbols, or symbolic forms, and leave the universal to look after itself. We think of the art-work as an image, or a particular pattern of imagery; the notion of the universal appears to be something derived as an abstract truth out of art-works rather than to be a deliberate aim embodied in them. At the very most we feel that the universal must necessarily be hidden in the concrete particulars of imagery and form, on which interest centres, and that these are always variants, the changing forms of whatever universal forces, essences, or principles may be alleged. Even the neo-classicist Pope's famous dictum about 'what oft was thought but ne'er so well expressed' allows for this variation in the vehicle, even though general ideas are being expressed.

There is one extremely simple reason why works must show originality. It is that there must be something new of some kind, because a work that has nothing novel is a repetition, or imitation. A work that uses again ideas previously used, and past language or forms, is superfluous. In fact a very large number of works (especially poems) can quickly be shown to be either conscious or unconscious imitations, as, for example, epigon poetry, or the commonplaces of the merely fashionable, or work that is just banal in subject, feeling, and form. For the banal in art is the known masquerading as new creation, and as the universal. We always understand such works quite easily; we are used to them and know what is in them. Many people like the comfort of the familiar, and hence such works are popular. Take the following poem, for example:

The Downs

Oh! the downs high to the cool sky;
And the feel of the sun-warmed moss;
And each cardoon, like a full moon,
Fairy-spun of the thistle floss;
And the beech grove, and a wood dove,

And the trail where the shepherds pass;
And the lark's song, and the wind song,
And the scent of the parching grass!

JOHN GALSWORTHY

The sentiments and diction of these verses are wholly derivative,
ultimately from romantic nature poetry of the nineteenth
century; there is also an affectation in the language that
imitates the spuriously poetic. By contrast, every genuine work
should at its first appearance look a little strange, and invite us
to contest with it for its secret.

We can take it as axiomatic that a good work will either say
something new, in the sense of having an original subject-
matter; or take an old subject or theme and handle it in a new
way. Dramatists have often done this with well-known subjects
like Antony and Cleopatra, Medea, Electra, Dido and Aeneas,
and so on. All art is discovery, and extension. It accompanies
historical change, the constantly changing conditions and
problems of human life, the new forms of society. It takes account of new knowledge, new ways of thinking, new ways of
reacting. If we think of it as principally a representation (mimesis), we see how it finds new objects to depict, or new aspects; if
as the expression of beliefs and values, we see how it expresses
changes of outlook, often long before people in general have
suspected them; if as emotional expression, we observe how it
conveys new patterns of feeling arising from change.

The problem for judgement is always how to recognize the
place of the good work between two false positions; on the one
side the tame derivative work which, just because it is a good
imitation, may look deceptively good; and, on the other side,
the specious work that may look good just because it looks new.
In other words, how do we know that a work is both new and
good?

One answer to this question is that critical assessment always
works with several criteria simultaneously, so that one does not
use the criterion of originality or novelty in a vacuum. The
simplest version of this is that a good subject is no use without
good technical presentation, or, vice versa, a good style is no use
without interesting matter. Something will be said later about
the balancing of criteria.

An answer more immediately relevant is that it is very rare for anything like *total* novelty to be at issue. The newness may lie in one aspect; in the subject, or the ideas, or the feelings, or the style and method, and it need not extend in any radical way to the other elements, though in all major innovations new forms, or variations of form, do usually accompany new subjects. But it is a fact of literary history that an outlook, or a group of themes, gets established, and the same happens with innovations of form, as with blank verse, tragedy, or the sonnet, or the symbolist method. We then observe mutation; and novelty by mutation is the most common form novelty takes. We observe it in the evolution of a general outlook over a period. Romantic poets in England and on the Continent, for instance, worked within a broad framework of generally accepted ideas, each producing, however, a personal variant with an element of originality, as may be seen by comparing the pantheism of Goethe with that of Wordsworth and Novalis. Equally the mutation may lie in the variation or extension of a method, as with the formal types mentioned above. Every dramatist or novelist gives a new twist to the possibilities of their form, even when working within an established tradition. Moreover, the techniques of art, the handling of the medium, the projection of new forms, the appropriate exploitation of the medium by variation and extension, are subject to general, impersonal judgement. The formal and technical innovations of Henry James, James Joyce, Ibsen, or Brecht, to cite very outstanding cases, are real, and in no way dependent on subjective reactions.

We thus accept novelty as a primary criterion, but only with due regard for subtlety in applying it. Novelty understood as a mutation or extension is the important feature. Certainly it is so for the problem of evaluation; if one applied the strictest logic, total newness, in subject and method of expression, would mean that one was deprived completely of criteria, because previous ones would be irrelevant, and that of novelty itself would become an empty principle.

Historically, of course, the modern acute sense of the unique form of every work had its roots in the idea of originality that emerged in later eighteenth-century poetics. It is characterized nowadays, it seems to me, not only by a rational acknowledgement of the creative extension to art and literature that every good new work brings, but by an anxiety; it is associated with the current puritanical form of belief in the autonomy of the art-work, which we have criticized above as exaggerated. This autonomy, taken in a radical sense, means that each work has its own law. Wolfgang Kayser, a well-known German supporter of this view, said sharply: 'Wir fragen, was das Werk sein will und messen es an ihm selber.'[1] This, in my view, oversimplifies, and is not true as it stands. The first stage of judgement, as we have just expounded, is to recognize quality. Now this we can only do by reference to a standard—that is to say, a conception of what a literary work is and looks like—and such a conception develops within our sensibility as we become familiar with good literature. When we read a work which is either quite new, or new at least for ourselves, we apply to it standards outside itself, criteria established in previous literature, both generally and in reference to specific genres or forms. In doing this we get the feeling that 'there is something in it', even though it may take us time to come to a fuller understanding. It is at the *second* stage of evaluation that we look at a work in the light of its own law. What we judge from the work itself is its individual character amongst other works. We expect it, in fact, to have an individual cast, and do not make the mistake of condemning it for being unlike other works. But we do this only after we have decided that it *is* an example of literary expression. We rely always on previous aesthetic–poetic experience, of which we must have a certain range to make a secure basis of judgement. The balancing of primary and secondary criteria is also important; the former operate always, the latter change from case to case, and person to person.

One aspect of the criterion of originality leads to misunderstandings and confused discussion. People often link the idea of the new with the idea of a predominant new contemporary feeling and style common to a number of writers of the same generation; they show a change of consciousness, as we say, which characterizes the new present as against preceding phases of style. Such changes, seen in a somewhat simplified perspective, are the materials of historical interpretation, being distinguished as significant periods. The fact that such changes

---

[1] 'We ask what the work aims to be, and measure it against itself.' 'Literarische Wertung und Interpretation', in *Die Vortragsreise* (Bern, 1958), p. 50.

do occur, and the habit of historical interpretation, dispose critics and others very easily to adopt the view that a writer who is any good at all *ought* to express his time', as is often said; or, in other words, he ought to be writing in such a way that later historians will be able to say that he was character-istic of what they deem to be the character of his period. Thus a factor of historical interpretation is transformed into a criterion.

This is an erroneous short-circuit and a crude simplification. A period is all sorts of things, and in no way just equivalent to one profiled view. There are many ways of being of one's age without necessarily fitting into one pattern. Art and poetry bring to consciousness new ways of thought and feeling, but many and varied ones, in currents and cross-currents, and they do so by virtue of the innocence and spontaneity in genuine artistic creation. It is the mark of the poet to be absolutely true to his feelings, intuitions, and insights, and to have the faculty of revealing them in language. It is a necessary and logical consequence that he expresses the life *he* feels and sees, which must be the life of today and not of yesterday, the life of his personal present. All good literature has this kind of contempor-ary authenticity; it is all of its time, and by its very nature expresses *some* aspect of its age. Being novel, and expressing some contemporary theme or feeling, does not mean that all authors at a given moment are lined up in chorus and speaking in unison. Nor that an author should feel an obligation con-sciously to look round, sum up for himself what the age is about, and 'express it'. You can make generalizations *ex post facto* about the literary productions of a given period but injunctions to writers are out of place. You could conceivably tell a writer to give a picture of something that has never been expressed before, as Flaubert told Maupassant to describe people and things in a different way from any previous; or as Yeats told Synge to go to the Western Isles and depict the peasants and fishermen there and the way they lived. But to tell a man to 'express his age', or to imply in criticism that this is what one expects, is to take hold of the wrong end of the stick. No one knows really what 'the age' is, or rather was, until it is past or passing, and its documentation well-nigh complete. Thomas Mann has said how in his earlier years he wrote without giving much thought to others or to the time, and only later did he realize that in speaking for himself he had also spoken for his contemporaries, and thus had been a representative voice without knowing it.

Another important point, which has been implied in the preceding paragraphs, is that novelty is intimately connected with individual style. Every authentic style is personal and therefore a new creation; and every significant poet or writer has his authentic style. This becomes established usually in a series of works. Here we come face to face with a cogent reason why evaluation must often go beyond the single work in order to function adequately and with security. What Henry James called the figure in the carpet, or Proust the song that inheres in a true style, both of which are largely determined by the unconscious and are guarantees of creative integrity, are relevant to the evaluation of each of a writer's works. Many good judges, for example, have withheld, or severely qualified, their admiration for Picasso because he has had so many styles. In his cubism, constructivism, neoclassicism, surrealism, etc., he was suspected of always imitating others for the want of a genuine line of his own. Amongst dramatists Cocteau has come in for the same kind of criticism. It may be mistaken or not, but it is at least symptomatic for the expectation we have that there is a close relation between new vision and authentic personal style.

It seems to me that a powerful psychological motive serves to support the importance of originality; indeed we may well see it as part of a biological-creative process if we look at the whole human, social, and cultural context of literature. We observe a continuing process not only of historical change but also of the simultaneous self-realization and self-imaging of man, in thought, art, and science, at every stage. This process or drive is most evident in the extreme egoism of the creative individual, where his particular work is concerned. It provides the inward drive towards an individual expression, towards doing something not done before, or not done before in the way now conceived. The historical fact corresponding to this powerful motive is that almost all poets and artists who maintain interest do so because of their having done something no one else thought of, *adding* to the stock of symbolized experience.

Thus the expectation, or demand, from the spectator, the recipient, for something novel joins hands with the egoistic pressure of the artistic impulse, and in this harmony the criterion of novelty gets firmly established.

12

THE BALANCING OF CRITERIA

We have considered some general criteria; first, the reference of a given work to reality, external man and nature, or the internal world of the psyche, which are the areas that provide the content of our experiences and our thought. We came to see that greater refinements in the manner of apprehending and interpreting both self and non-self lead to a position where we have to rely on a sense of truth, or sincerity, or possibility of meaning, in order to assess difficult exploratory work positively. Secondly, we distinguished philosophical awareness, or, in other words, the sense of genuine problems, a seriousness of content (even in the midst of comedy), that raises work above triviality or the commonplace. Thirdly, we analysed more closely the criterion of unity, unified effect, organic wholeness, and formulated the notion of metaphorical unity, which, furthermore, we saw as effective in conjunction with compositional unity. Fourthly, we considered novelty, or originality, and saw this as an aspect of the extension of realized experience, and we associated it with sincerity and authenticity.

These criteria do not depend on particular beliefs or philosophies, nor on verse or prose, nor on kinds or formal types. All these bedevil the problem of primary judgement, because they introduce such enormous variety into literary products. This variety, moreover, as we expounded in Part I, extends to critical reception; many good critics work with sets of criteria that indicate a taste, not a universally valid basis of judgement. But the criteria examined above are, in my view, quite central to judgement and therefore primary; every work must be referred to them, whatever further qualities, values, or criteria may be involved.

But let us reaffirm at this point an observation made at the outset. It cannot be too often emphasized that in making judgements the decisive thing is not one quality or feature but a group of qualities interacting and in balance. Enthusiastic, clinching generalizations, such as that literature reveals the universal, or essential reality, or the hidden truth of things, may suggest conceptions that are not irrelevant; but certain it is that they cannot be clues to judgement. They cannot, as unproved terms, be criteria. Moreover, taken too absolutely, they do not allow for the enormous variety of literary expression, in respect of both subject-matter and tone, from the most sublime to the lightest and most capricious. Similarly, some leading ideas from aesthetics, such as Schopenhauer's use of Platonic forms, or Croce's intuition and expression, or current notions of symbolization, do not provide criteria. Aesthetic principles in themselves are inductive generalizations based on judgements already made about selected examples taken to be art. Some well-known terms of the New Criticism, such as Ransom's local texture, Brooks's irony, Tate's tension, Burke's symbolic action, or Blackmur's gesture, are put forward as critical principles and instruments of evaluation, but they are in fact nearer to aesthetic explanatory ideas than to criteria in the strict sense. Perhaps this is why it is often said, now that these new principles have fallen into a theoretical perspective, that their authors were good critics in spite of theory, because they 'were intelligent', more concrete, local, and particular, and not shackled by their abstract principles.

To perform the act of evaluation we have to look for a decisive pattern in which certain features and qualities are co-present, interfused, and intricate. There must be a representation of something within human experience, and of human interest, mimetic and cognitive, or emotional and expressive, or both. There must be unity, a harmonious, concordant whole, but made of the right elements, and metaphorical in texture, not barely architectonic. There must be a worthy theme, an informing idea, some 'philosophical awareness', the play of the mind with its varied qualities and gifts on the material, if banality and triviality are to be avoided; but the presentation is by image, symbol, and form, and with adherent emotion. There must be novelty and discovery, original ways of seeing and speaking being the sign of authenticity and sincerity; but not every aspect of a work need be equally new. There must, let us add, be technical power, craftsmanship, command of an apparatus (language, imagery, fictional invention, etc.) because, in the first place, this distinguishes the real artist from the inarticulate visionary or naïve dreamer; and, in the second, because the use of such an apparatus is the instrument of imagination and helps to make the superabundance, as against the utility, of expression; but it must be dovetailed with meanings, and not be simply empty play or mere pattern. Every good literary work satisfies these principal criteria simultaneously; it is the co-presence of the basic features that is decisive. This was referred to briefly above in connection with novelty. Novelty alone can be mere modishness; expressive feeling alone can be vacuous, pointless; an interesting thought or idea alone remains a pedantic or staid statment; unity alone can be external and rigid, and so on. It is when the features are in harmonious interfusion that the poetic realization takes place. Works are correspondingly imperfect when the conditions are only partially fulfilled, and they are not then necessarily wholly bad or without interest.

The application of the criteria discussed, and which are here called primary, in their interrelationship is in my view an objective process, independent of purely subjective impressions or responses. They are independent of taste, and of taste and judgement based on sets of specific criteria, as described above (cf. pp. 54-5). They enable poetic and literary quality to be acknowledged without the involvement of like or dislike.

13

CRITERIA AND THE PROBLEM OF HISTORICAL UNDERSTANDING

NOT many thinking people would nowadays deny that historical knowledge can change one's view of a poetic work, and help, as is said, to create a better understanding of it; and most people would sympathize with the persuasive plea put forward for the historical approach by Helen Gardner in *The Business of Criticism*. On the whole we can say that historical criteria belong to detailed, expert evaluation rather than to primary judgement, since they are normally only brought to bear on works that were originally judged to be in fact of literary value. It is when works no longer exercise the same obvious and immediate attraction that one looks to history to justify them. But although redemption by historical illumination seems straightforward, the relations between aesthetic and historical factors are in fact extremely intricate and difficult. The appeal to historical evidence does not give an actual criterion; it only provides, at the best, a better *basis* for judgement. It shows you the gates of a past poetic region, opens them, but you may still remain outside, able only to gaze into foreign property. Finally, historical knowledge simply restores past appreciation, and makes it once more into a norm. But again, the idea that historical knowledge inevitably increases aesthetic understanding or enjoyment is not necessarily always true. It can work the other way round, as in the example from Kleist quoted later in this chapter, where the uncovered historical points of view are unattractive and repugnant as against the psychological interest which is contemporary in temper (cf. p. 130).

The situation we are bound to accept now, at least with readers who have any general education at all, is that the extreme positions are no longer possible; we certainly cannot revert to a past or period situation, converting ourselves into past men, but neither can we be quite naïve about the works from the past. Our education gives us a sense of history, which, once acquired, is not easy to lose or shake off. A very little experience of reading classics of literature, moreover, makes one naturally look for historical alignments and traditions. In practice we inherit a load of habits and previous assessments. It is not at all easy to be quite innocent. On the other hand we cannot so immerse ourselves in a past situation, even with the help of the most detailed historical knowledge, that we could reconstitute the aesthetic experiences germane to it as though we were contemporaries. We cannot become Elizabethans and feel Marlowe and Shakespeare quite as they did, nor can we feel the response to poetic pantheism in the way the late eighteenth century did. We must also admit that if past works could only be enjoyed, or found interesting, at the cost of a mass of detailed historical knowledge, and with the feeling even then of only approximate identification, we should soon be finding the price too high.

So we cannot be either completely historical or completely contemporary, but have to acknowledge a complex relationship between the two. What this is, or can be, is difficult to pin down. It is not enough to think of accepted art as permanently valid. ' "All good art is contemporary" is a well-known critical maxim', writes Helen Gardner, adding the counterstatement that all art is also historical.[1] But there is a third term, the a-historical, which is not the same as the contemporary, or the vaguely universal. We must avoid the trap of thinking that, because a work is finished at a particular historical moment, it is at that moment new and part of an instantaneous 'present', after which it is historical, an incident of 'the past'. This pre-supposes a grossly simple view of the way works come into being. They are not incidents or occurrences in time as events, or our actions, are; they are thought about, often over long periods of time, months or years, worked out, constructed, written, re-written, revised; they may contain elements of immediate experience in the present, but they are also made with mental materials, given by memory, reason, observation, and imagination, that are a-temporal, outside chronology, available from stock at any time. A finished work is a fusion of

[1] *The Business of Criticism* (Oxford, 1959), p. 17.

all these things together.[1] The psychological processes of meaning-construction, and of a range of aesthetic qualities (pertaining to sensuous or formal beauty), which belong to this situation, are permanent human characteristics, biologically and physiologically conditioned. We remember also that perception processes in general, and our apprehension of meanings, depend on schematic and *Gestalt*-operations, and not on the literal apprehension of concrete details in their totality; and that language itself, jumping detail, functions in schematic ways. In consequence past works are not all necessarily more remote or difficult for the understanding than present ones, if we consider them all as versions of a third thing, namely a relation of man to concrete reality.

Factors of this kind are the natural basis for a-historical understanding of literary creations. By virtue of them we can still have, for instance, some appreciation of Minoan art or Greek verse; and keeping them in mind it is easy to see that the idea of a work being simply the product of a given historical situation, or moment, or set of circumstances, is crude and inadequate. It has some a-historical character built in from the start.

We must find a different way of conceiving our relationship with past works. It is not a simple line from the present to a point in the past, as though one were to let a film run in reverse; not a groping from contemporary consciousness backwards to an unfamiliar one in the past. Another connection, another line of communication, exists, which side-tracks simple regression, and passes instead via the a-historical. In other words, the a-historical elements in all our thinking, and in our artistic activity (creation and reception), speak to the a-historical

---

[1] E. Vivas and M. Krieger include in *The Problems of Aesthetics* (New York, 1953) a passage from Henri Matisse, *Notes of a Painter*, which illumines this point: 'Both harmonies and dissonances of colour can produce very pleasurable effects. Often when I settle down to work I begin by noting my immediate and superficial colour sensation. Some years ago this first was often enough for me—but today if I were satisfied with this my picture would remain incomplete. I would have put down the passing sensations of a moment; they would not completely define my feelings and the next day I might not recognize what they meant. I want to reach that state of condensation of sensations which constitutes a picture. Perhaps I might be satisfied momentarily with a work finished at one sitting but I would soon get bored looking at it; therefore, I prefer to continue working on it so that later I may recognize it as a work of my mind' (pp. 256–7).

elements in past works. We can allow, moreover, for numerous patterns in this relationship. Clearly, using detailed historical knowledge, one can stress the historically valid features of a work, its embeddedness in the past; alternatively one can stress the a-historical features so as to lift it out of time; and the two interpretations evolved in this way will differ. The main point at the present juncture is to stress the plural patterns of relationship, and avoid basing the problem on absolutes of theory like the old notion of universality or of Platonic type, or supratemporal ideality. We can say, in fact, that we need both relationships to history, the one in which it is stressed, and the other in which it does not obtrude or seem important. We need the sense, if not of absolute universality, at least of the long authority of outstanding works or styles, of something deeply rational or far-reachingly human that is consistent and continuous; but also, on the other hand, the sense of difference and change, of personal and historical individuality, of the flow of time and things, because it is in their nature to flow.

This seems to me to offer a more fruitful approach nowadays than any attempt to keep alive dubious criteria like permanence. The latter is not really a criterion, but an *ex post facto*, automatic confirmation of original judgements. The term is also inaccurate. It suggests continuing, equal validity, at all times and in all places; whereas what happens usually with a work and the 'history of its repute' is a waxing and waning as circumstances and taste change. A dominant constellation of belief and aesthetic preferences in a particular period effects a change of relationships with the past; it is a parallel in group reactions to the constellations creating personal taste as discussed in Part I.

Literary works have notoriously a certain ambiguity, and are the richer for it. One result is variability in interpretations. Connected with this is a quality which may be called resonance, a consequence of which in the subsequent history and reputation of a work is that latent possibilities of meaning unfold themselves as time goes on; for art-works share with real human beings, in their life-processes in time, the inexhaustible mystery of living things. But another cause of resonance is the density or generality of their symbolism and references. By virtue of these a work retains its effective truth in spite of changed historical circumstances, or the historical distance of new readers, as happens in the case of Shakespearean tragedy. But another possibility is that time can change the priorities of interpretation or simply add new meanings. A striking example is Ibsen's *A Doll's House*. When it appeared, this play received greatest acclamation as a programmatic piece about feminine emancipation; when Nora slammed the door of her sham home defiantly behind her, husbands and wives, as was said, heard the bang reverberate through the whole of Europe. The stark power of *A Doll's House* as a *pièce-à-thèse* has been dissipated by time; but the character delineation and the psychology are so substantial that the piece comes off today even better as an exemplary portrayal of a crisis of self-scrutiny and self-discovery leading to an act of liberation and a new beginning in the hard but salutary glare of truth.

An example of the greatest interest is Kleist's *Der Prinz von Homburg*. In the Germany of the nineteenth century, from the overthrow of the national enemy Napoleon to Bismarck and the Wilhelminian empire, this play was consistently interpreted in the sense of Prussianism and nationalism. The Prince is court-martialled by the King as military commander-in-chief for disobeying battle orders and jeopardizing the whole plan of action; the punishment for the offence is death. The incredulous Prince, who is in fact pleased with himself and his successful independent manœuvre, is forced to re-think the problem of military discipline in its relation to the state and patriotic duty, and through a moral purge is brought to full recognition of his misdemeanour and to a willing acceptance of the stern but appropriate penalty. The King then exercises his clemency. This play was commonly quoted as *Das Hohelied preussischen Soldatentums;* moreover one looked upon the firm ethic as a sign that Kleist, after a series of wildly passionate, irrational, and unorthodox plays, was at last reaching poetic maturity. Yet the recent international interest in the play, its production in France and England, can scarcely be ascribed to its being the Song of Songs of Prussian militarism. Nowadays it is Kleist's uncanny psychological clairvoyance that the modern reader appreciates. In the nineteenth century the critics who took the patriotic line condemned Kleist's addiction to somnambulism, transvestism, hysterias of erotic origin, and morbid psychological states in general; such features were blemishes. Today, the position is reversed; the history, the patriotism, the State, the military order, are all tolerated as the mere framework for the really important thing, the psychology. Nevertheless, if one does take account of history, if one does appreciate the moment of genesis as a historical situation, one has to admit that the patriotic interpretation is possible. The time was 1810; Kleist was co-operating vigorously with leading writers and statesmen in the marshalling of all the defences of the country against the invader Napoleon. In these circumstances we cannot deny that the nineteenth-century interpretation was valid; we can simply add another, which at the present time displaces the former without in any proper sense invalidating it.

These are two very marked examples of works with latent meanings brought out much later in time, and illustrating the triangular scheme of past, present, and a-historical, which has to be invoked to account for the intricate relationship of past works to the present, and the difficulty of applying historical criteria.

If we accept this position it is clear that a further complication is added to the concept of 'history of literature'. To admit an a-historical factor in the very inception of a work is to restrict the idea of historical siting and progression, though it is only one element of the case. But this is not our immediate problem, which concerns the bearing of historical factors on evaluation. Here the important thing is that there should be a fruitful relationship between the historical and the a-historical. If historical knowledge leads to an enhancement of the poetic experience, we are properly within the area of the aesthetic. If not, aesthetic values fade out and we are simply historians of past writing.

14

MORAL CRITERIA

THE problem of a moral standard for literary works, a kind of passport or certificate of hygiene, arises from the simple fact that poems and fictions, being representations of life, extend to all its diversity and inevitably include subjects that arouse moral judgements, as they do in actual life. There are especially two cases that focus the problem; one is the book of which some people will say that it is an immoral book, like *Fanny Hill*, or the *Decameron*, because of bawdy subject-matter; the other is the book, like *Lady Chatterley's Lover*, that contravenes not morality itself but the current orthodoxy of a particular society.

No one can deny that world literature of a high standard can disclose a fair quantity of morally suspect materials. Early examples are the sexual habits on Olympus and the ranking of character traits in Homeric heroes. Even in Milton's Christian epic the bad but heroic Satan wins more admiration and sympathy than the radiant purity of the cherubic orders. It is a paradox of allegories that they have to depict wickedness and vice in vivid, intense, alluring colours in order to show precisely the degree of temptation involved, especially when it is to sensual pleasure, as well as to throw better into relief the triumph of virtue; but which bits are most read and enjoyed? The art of the poet arouses more passionate involvement in the dramatic detail than in the abstract moral triumph on the final page. We remember a long tradition of eroticism in distinguished literature, and the role of adultery in innumerable romances and novels. The picaresque novel, the novel of adventure, and the comedy of manners, have all contributed to vicarious temptation, not to mention the lower and the higher decadence of the *fin-de-siècle*, and the progressive disappearance of most of the taboos in this century.

Moral objections in extreme form come, of course, from religion, especially from severe Protestants and Nonconformists who are ethics-dominated. Puritanism is the potentially fanatic enemy because of its attitude to pleasure. If you think all pleasure is basically sinful it is only logical to suspect aesthetic pleasure, even without obvious lewdness. A modified form of the pleasure-is-sin belief is that pleasures may be divided into pure and impure; immoral elements in art then come under the second head. Some religious people take the view that true literature is only possible in harmony with the principles and dogmas of their religion; but this is not quite the same thing as holding all other literature to be immoral.

Another view, less extreme than the above but also severe, is discussed by Wimsatt.[1] He adduces the case of the engineer who, whatever his aesthetic ambition, may not build a bridge that he cannot guarantee to be strong enough for its purpose; and the case of the chef, also a kind of artist, who may not provide gustatory beauty in the form of food gone bad. And the point is made that a poet likewise may not present a work, however beautiful, that he knows will have a corrupting influence. The great difference between such examples and literature is, of course, that the one is an actual physical hazard on the sinking bridge, or with the poisonous food, and the other an imponderable moral hazard which can only be theoretically alleged and rarely proven in fact. The strictest enforcement of the idea of anticipating a possible danger, and ensuring protection against it, would shackle literature intolerably. Logically it would mean that only morally acceptable materials should be used, and even, if protection is to be adequately ensured, that an open moral purpose must be always apparent. For the extreme attitude, we must remember, there is no innocent area at all where subject-matter and thoughts are unaffected by moral judgements; what is not moral is immoral or anti-moral. This is really the position that Tolstoy arrived at.

The religious hostility to literature, or large parts of it, is at least respectably based on sincerely held principles, even though a puritanical excess may sometimes seem to disfigure it. Less well founded, and more spectacular, is the attack made by the guardians of a conventional or institutional morality, which is usually that of a particular society or national community; it is the phenomenon of 'public morality', which is maintained by the State and its laws acting in accordance with a real or

<hr />

[1] W. K. Wimsatt, Jr., *The Verbal Icon* (New York, 1964), p. 90.

supposed majority view. Great mischief is done here because the issue is muddled. The attack on immorality from morality is given a subtle twist; it becomes simply an allegation of immorality from a different moral position, or an externally accepted moral view. The moral itself is then in dispute, and the conflict shifts to socio-political ground and the implementation of standard conventions. The State then talks morality to mask its real aims; it has no real interest in what literature is, but only in the possible effects of particular works on its citizens, and the effects it means are sometimes moral in the narrow sense, but often such as are insurrectionary or critical of the *status quo*. This socio-political intervention was very marked in Europe in the later nineteenth century, which brought great activity to the censorships in various countries. The new drama of Ibsen, with disciples like Shaw and Brieux, was an example of how a powerful influence could in fact be exerted on the public by literature, simple because an attack was seen to be made directly on vulnerable targets of social morality; and, as we know, special theatres were organized in London, Paris, and Berlin for the performance of censored plays. Hauptmann and Wedekind also suffered at the hands of the police and the authorities. In the field of the novel we remember the flagrant cases of *Madame Bovary*, *Ulysses*, and *Lady Chatterley's Lover*, against which a lawsuit was brought thirty years after the death of its author. But these *causes célèbres* represent only the salient points of public demonstration; all the time, only less dramatically concentrated, the moral opposition is maintained.

We have to remember in this connection an important function of literature. It has become an accepted tradition since the eighteenth century for literature to undertake, amongst other things, an inquiry into man's socio-political conditions of existence; and actual morality, under the resulting analysis, has been seen much more than previously as a consequence of social conditions and class rather than as the ideal application of rationally deduced, universal moral principles. Literature has espoused the causes of humanity against all forms of oppression, deception, illusion, and specious morality. It has in consequence been in conflict more and more continuously with established authorities and conventional moral codes; and the reaction of the latter, in defence of their *status quo*, has been to hit back with the blanket charge of immorality and sedition. But literature has acted in the name of truth, and freedom of thought, and freedom to criticize. In this situation, honour lies in the accusation of subversion, or immorality, or anti-religion; because the challenge to moral ideas is always itself moral when made in good faith, arising as it does from an ideal of freedom, happiness, and human fulfilment. Notably Ibsen is saturated with this kind of moral anti-morality. Literature generally has staked out a claim to be one agent of a continuing process of emancipation, in which illusions and false truth are constantly unmasked and replaced by more adequate truths and moral conceptions.

It is clear from a few indications of this kind that the problem of the morality or immorality of literature is a real one that goes beyond private pre-occupation and touches public life. A defence of literature which may include doubtful materials is necessary. The immediate question for us, in the context of the primary criteria of judgement, is whether a moral criterion in a particular sense is either relevant or appropriate.

Approaching first from aesthetics, it is not difficult to find a logical justification for the moral neutrality of the aesthetic sphere. Kant promulgated the idea of disinterested pleasure. Following him Schopenhauer set aesthetic experience apart from the practical sphere of the Will, representing it as a condition of contemplation, through which man could withdraw from the aggressive self-assertion of the will-dominated ego. In this century another example of this kind of distinction between aesthetic and moral, or practical, is to be seen in Croce's view of art as intuition, which is distinct from logic on the one hand, and moral action on the other. Theories such as these make the aesthetic experience one of total detachment in contemplation, in which one is freed from passionate involvement. They provide a basis for the frequently expressed explanation of why disagreeable subjects in art nevertheless give pleasure; it is because the treatment, not the subject, is the source of pleasure.

Certainly it can be safely held that literary art, considered simply as *mimesis*, is morally neutral. It is a way of showing things, and therein lies a value; but it can show both good and bad things. Things that are the objects of passionless seeing are unreal; they are taken up into thought and imagination and have then an ideal meaning. This is the case as long as one holds strictly to a pure representation. From this point of view one cannot bring the charge of immorality against any subject-matter treated in this way. Art can reveal very vividly things that in other contexts would be immoral; lust, evil motives, and blatant sensuality. But the object is different from the process; in the representation it becomes idea, and the revealing in itself is not immoral. It is a statement, not an action that can be judged by moral principles. In other words, art does not change morality or moral truth, nor our moral judgements, or way of making them. Any moral elements in poetic works we judge by the canons of ethical principle, or our belief in moral intuitions. No artistic or poetic power can change something judged morally wrong into a right; what it does is to reveal with equal vividness and style both good and bad. But the intensely or stylishly revealed bad is still bad, as any other object or aspect of life in a mimesis remains itself as the object of the representation.

I think it is true to say that the aesthetic of truth, or a belief in the cognitive validity of art, is one of the most widespread assumptions in the literature and art of the present age. As we saw in Part I it has displaced the notion of literature as edification, and also, in the last two decades, the idea of expression and self-expression; or at least it has provided an intellectual containing force against undisciplined or sentimental expressive activity. In this fusion of truth and aesthetic lies, in my view, the essential moral justification of much twentieth-century literature that uses on a large scale, and with conscious aim, materials and themes that were offensive and taboo in preceding periods. It is the assumption also on which criticism relies, though more by implication than by open admission.

The relation between literature and morals must in fact be conceived on these or similar broader lines if it is to do equal justice to the amoral character of aesthetic seeing and to an ulterior, believed harmony between aesthetic and extra-aesthetic values, including the moral. The relation, in other words, cannot be expressed in terms of a particular criterion, such as: does the work accord with moral principles? Morality in the crude sense is a non-criterion; a moral sensibility, how-ever, is a background presence. For the act of evaluation the case is covered in my view by our criterion of philosophical awareness, as well as by the inclusiveness of judgement that takes account simultaneously of several factors in balance. The portrayal of evil or lewdness for its own sake, which would be a corruptive influence, would offend the philosophical and sincere sense of human values, and it would upset the balance of true inclusive judgement. One could put this another way by saying that apparent immorality in the materials of parts of a work is corrected in the philosophical perspective of the whole; so that a part may in isolation appear to be suspect, but the work as a whole is not. What will not do here, I think, is to distinguish too simply between the 'art' and the subject represented; this is a specious distinction for judgement, because the meaning of 'art' is here restricted to mimetic technique, whereas what judgement is concerned with is a total poetic statement.

The boundary of the immoral is reached when use, or application, or motivation, change the potential aesthetic experience into a behavioural pattern. This can happen on the receiving side, when a reader detaches sections of a work from their context and gloats over them for their own sake, as with brutality, or evil, or sensuality, or whatever, without regard to their proper significance within the comprehensive meaning of the whole work. He then creates pornography for himself. It happens also on the author's side when he deliberately aims to create an effect on his reader which is real, putting him into a state of corrupt feeling and desire; the author, this time, creates the pornography. Real feelings and real physical involvement supervene, and the aesthetic experience is destroyed.

It is thus the *use* of mimesis, and the motive, that are decisive. Mimesis, if it is the deliberately infectious expression of corrupt desires, is degraded by motive; it is put to service and becomes part of an action. It is used for real individual satisfactions of an immoral kind. It is in this area that public intervention for the protection of minors, who do not fully understand the issues, may well be justified. Unfortunately the motives of those who tend to intervene are not always quite reasonable or pure.

Finally, a brief comment should be made on the vacillations of moral judgements themselves; moral codes and ideals are not constant but subject to change. In consequence there must quite frequently be distortions in the pattern of judgement when moral and aesthetic factors are simultaneously involved. A public taste that is related to a public morality is in danger from time; notions of what is morally acceptable change almost with each generation. What was forbidden yesterday is permitted today; what is accepted today, let us add, may be forbidden tomorrow. Then authors and their works come into their own again, according to their affinity with the age. The Victorian puritans expurgated the *Decameron*; our later age gives, as a fruit of emancipation, positive moral value to what previously was condemned.

INDEX

affinity, criticism of, 21, 45, 48, 50,
52; *see also* debate, criticism of
literature of, 17–21, 22, 26, 36–7,
40, 48, 60–1, 64–5
affirmation, literature as, 27–8, 103;
see also functions of literature
Aiken, H. D., 30n.
Aristotle, 22, 82, 86
Arnold, Matthew, 34, 58, 61, 114
assessment, criticism as, 45, 49,
51–2, 55–6, 69, 72–3, 78, 83, 117,
127
Austen, Jane, 64
autonomy of art, 15–16, 24–5, 33,
38, 101, 119, 135

Babbitt, Irving, 59, 74–5
Bach, J. S., 102
Bacon, F., 60
Baudelaire, Charles, 105
Beckett, Samuel, 94, 104
Bell, C., 26
Blackmur, R. P., 33, 62, 124
Boileau, Nicolas, 81
Bos, C. du, 40
Brecht, Bertold, 35, 43–4, 97, 118
Brieux, E. 134
Brooks, C., 30, 113n., 124
Browning, Robert, 6
Brunetière, F., 7, 75
Büchner, G., 43–4
Bunyan, John, 35, 96, 100
Burke, K., 124
Butler, Samuel, 43
Byron, Lord George, 41, 113

Casey, John, 54–5
catharsis, 22–3, 61
Chekhov, Anton, 101
classics of literature, 4–5, 49, 58–61,
85, 115–16, 127
Claudel, P., 64, 98, 100
Cocteau, Jean, 121

Coleridge, S. T., 51
Collingwood, R. G., 15
Compton-Burnett, Ivy, 64
criteria of judgement, *see* judgement
criticism, practical, v, 4; *see also*
Richards
Croce, B., 25n., 71, 124, 135
cultural criticism, 31, 40, 56–7, 62
curiosity, and attitudes to literature,
17–21, 48, 102

Dante Alighieri, 26, 33, 40, 42
debate, criticism of, 21, 45, 48–51;
see also affinity, criticism of
Dickens, Charles, 6
Donne, John, 26, 99
Dryden, John, 43

education and literature, 17, 38–9,
48, 58–65
Eliot, T. S., 23, 27–9, 37, 42, 50–4,
61n., 76–7, 81, 98–100, 106
Emerson, R. W., 40
evaluation, 3–6, 16, 34, 42, 45–7,
49, 50 2, 54–5, 57, 69, 73–85, 95,
98–9, 112–14, 118–19, 121, 124,
126, 131, 136–7; *see also* judgement
Evans, Joan, 61n.
explication, criticism of, 49–50, 52,
78, 82
expression, literature as, 16–17, 19,
27–8, 30, 32, 40, 44, 47, 87–91,
93–4, 100, 103–5, 117, 124–5,
136; *see also* functions of literature

Flaubert, Gustave, 120, 134
Fry, R., 26
functions of literature, v, 3, 14, 17,
20, 22–44 *passim*, 45, 58–60, 97–8,
134

Galsworthy, John, 84, 116–17
Gardner, Helen, 80, 126–7